The OPTIMUM KAYAK

The OPTIMUM KAYAK

How to Choose, Maintain, Repair, and Customize the Right Boat for You

Andy Knapp

Ragged Mountain Press / McGraw-Hill
Camden, Maine • New York • San Francisco • Washington, D.C. • Auckland •
Bogotá • Caracas • Lisbon • London • Madrid • Mexico City • Milan •
Montreal • New Delhi • San Juan • Singapore • Sydney • Tokyo • Toronto

Ragged Mountain Press
A Division of The McGraw-Hill Companies

10 9 8 7 6 5 4 3 2 1

Library of Congress Cataloging-in-Publication Data
Knapp, Andy, 1947–
    The optimum kayak : how to choose, maintain, repair, and customize the right boat for you / Andy Knapp.
        p.   cm.
    Includes bibliographical references (p.   ) and index.
    ISBN 0-07-038298-0 (alk. paper)
    1. Kayaks. 2. Kayaking.   I. Title.
GV783.K62   1999
797.1'224—dc21   99-32854
                                                              CIP

Questions regarding the content of this book should be addressed to
Ragged Mountain Press
P.O. Box 220
Camden, ME 04843
http://www.raggedmountainpress.com

Questions regarding the ordering of this book should be addressed to
The McGraw-Hill Companies
Customer Service Department
P.O. Box 547
Blacklick, OH 43004
Retail customers: 1-800-262-4729
Bookstores: 1-800-722-4726

This book is printed on 70# Citation.

Drawings by Matt Kania.
Photographs by the author unless otherwise indicated.

Printed by Quebecor, Fairfield, PA
Design by Madhouse Studios
Project management by Janet Robbins
Page layout by Shannon Thomas
Edited by Tom McCarthy and Rob Lawson

To my father, who encouraged my earliest travels
by bicycle and got me started on the road to adventure.

Contents

Acknowledgments

As with any major project, many people have made contributions, directly or indirectly, as the ideas came together. I am indebted to my many friends and contacts in the paddlesports industry: Wil Bryan, Dagger sales rep; Lili and Gordon Colby, Mad River/Voyageurs; Joe Dryden, Eddyline Kayaks; Mojo Rogers, Werner Paddles; and Cheryl Willis, McNett Outdoor; among others, who provided information and assistance.

I have had the opportunity over the years to know and work with some key players in the world of kayaking who were generous with their wisdom or support for my endeavors, including: Ken Fink, Tom and Lisa Derrer, Stan and Ema Chladek, Frank Goodman, Brian Henry, Steve Scarborough, Steve Omeara, Bruce Furrer, and Jerry Lloyd. And I would like to thank my friends at *Canoe & Kayak* magazine who got me started on the Workshop columns that became the inspiration for this book.

Thanks also to paddling friends Chuck Holst, John Andrew, and Steve Gougeon. Dale Hedtke, owner of the Boat-House in St. Paul, provided valuable assistance with wooden kayak issues. And of course many ideas have been fermenting since the days of paddling with good friend "Bivouac" Pete Roy.

After a year of participating in the internet mailing list, I've found Paddlewise to be a source of ideas and opinions that have reinforced some of my own good ideas and shot down the bad ones (see the Paddlewise listing in chapter 8, Resources). A free exchange of ideas will only continue to benefit our sport.

And finally, the patience, and sometimes impatience, of my family has made this work possible and driven it to completion.

Introduction

For billions of years, water has run across the surfaces of our planet, collecting into pools, streams, and rivers, then finding its way to the wind-blown seas and oceans. Everywhere along these waterways and coastlines this water lashes against the edges of the land, creating constant change and spawning the life that teems everywhere. Deep within our genetic makeup is something that draws us back to the water, whether it is to drink, to swim, to contemplate, or to stand in awe of the vast power of it in motion.

Few outdoor sports provide such unique lure at so many different levels as kayaking and paddlesports. Travel by kayak is tied to history and tradition, and it opens up a unique opportunity to enjoy and observe the natural environment. It gives the paddler an opportunity to develop and extend the boundaries of personal skills within the context of a group cooperative effort. Paddlesports provide communities with a connection to their local resources and heritage, adding an economic incentive for environmental protection. In short, it is a sport in which all of a person's abilities, mental as well as physical, work together to safely achieve a goal.

To outside observers, kayaking might be classified as a "thrill" sport, and in many ways it is. We can seek the thrill of accomplishment on the edge of danger, and we can find the thrill of discovery on the water and inside ourselves, but there's more to it than that. In the last decade or so, there has been a rapid growth of participation in all facets of kayaking. Whatever the motivation, be it excitement, adventure, discovery, escape, exercise, contemplation, few activities generate as much passion as among its adherents.

As well, few sports provide such an active spectrum of friendly disagreement. If you get two or more avid paddlers together for more than a minute, it is likely there will be a lively exchange of ideas on some paddling topic. There are many good introductory and advanced kayaking books that focus on skills and safety and provide a general overview of a particular branch of the sport. What sets this work apart is its practical bent, its insider's focus on the kayak itself and the related accessories necessary for the sport.

I grew up in Minnesota, a state where water recreation is the top draw, with an active love for the outdoors. I have paddled over 8,000 miles in many locations from the Everglades to coastal Alaska. Besides my hands-on experience with kayaks in a variety of settings and water conditions, I bring an insider's knowledge of outdoor equipment, having worked professionally in the industry.

My goal here is to provide information that will give paddlers, as they grow into the sport of kayaking, a good background in how they can expect their kayak and gear to perform in the field, what can be done to keep these things working well, and to suggest ways to fit the gear to individual needs. This book goes beyond the basics of just choosing products: it gives you the know-how to keep your kayak and accessories fine-tuned and in optimum service to meet *your* paddling needs. By optimizing your kayak, you will get more satisfaction out of the sport and more out of your investment in expensive gear by making it work correctly and helping it last longer.

There will be differences of opinion and alternative ways of accomplishing the same objectives. There always are, and that's fine. I hope to hear from readers at some point about a better way to do something, or that I overlooked some particular issue. Then I'll know that I have stimulated thought or added something to the debate.

Many of the issues concerning equipment, customizing, and outfitting kayaks are similar for most variations of the sport, from whitewater to sea kayaking. We will review this spectrum of the world of kayaks and kayaking gear, and then discuss how to get started in the area that interests you. Next, we will look in detail at three major areas of optimization: care and maintenance of your kayak and gear; basic repairs and fix-it projects; and ideas for customizing your kayak and gear to make it work for you. Additional chapters will focus on cartopping issues, portaging, other do-it-yourself projects, and resources for further information. Unless otherwise indicated, all prices are quoted in U.S. currency.

I have had the opportunity to learn a lot of things the hard way and to work with many great people in the paddlesports community. By sharing with you some of the ideas and knowledge about kayaking I have picked up over the years, I hope that you the paddler will find your time on the water to be more productive and enjoyable.

From here on, we will be talking about gear—all those flashy kayaks and all the neat gear and nifty gadgets—but remember that the most important gear, or gears, are the ones in your head. Kayaking is a sport of judgment; it's as much a mental game as a physical one. All the good gear in the world won't keep you out of trouble if you don't take the time to practice the skills, learn to read the water and the weather, and have the sense to apply what you know to the changing conditions. Those skills you won't get from a book—to get those you have to get out there and do it.

1
KAYAKING'S
BROAD SPECTRUM

Since its origins as a hunting and transportation craft in the indigenous cultures of the polar regions, people have adopted and adapted the kayak during the twentieth century into one of the most, if not *the most*, popular of human-powered recreational boats. Kayaks have poked around on innumerable lakes, descended most of the world's rivers, and explored large sections of the saltwater coastlines. Normally thought of as a decked craft propelled from a sitting position low in the hull by a double-bladed paddle, there are exceptions to these defining characteristics. Today's kayaks include a colorful band of decked canoes of various sorts, deckless sit-on-top and inflatable kayaks, and the use of single-bladed paddles. All of which can blur the most basic definition. What counts, however, is that this book's ideas and concepts are relevant to the broad range of paddle-craft generally referred to as kayaks.

The Long and Short of It

Once paddlers realized the recreational potential of kayaks, especially after the development of portable folding kayaks in Central Europe in the early 1900s, they took to the rivers, lakes, canals, and seashores, and their boats evolved into a vast number of models. To make sense of the diversity of today's variety of kayaks, imagine this array as a pyramid of stacked kayaks, the shorter models at the top. In general, short kayaks are more maneuverable but slower than long models and are used for shorter distances and more technical paddling. Long kayaks track better and cover distances more efficiently than short versions but won't maneuver as easily. Keeping these parameters in mind, you can understand potential strengths and weaknesses of particular kayaks and why they are used, and you can better assess what type of kayak is best for you.

The sport's extreme cutting edge manifests itself on either end of the kayak spectrum, and toward the center, more mainstream, recreational uses abound. Breaking loose with abundant energy at the short kayak end is the world of extreme whitewater paddling, of waterfall jumping and wilderness first descents, of pushing the boundaries, daring to do the impossible. Driven by adrenaline, kayakers in this class have high levels of skills and are willing to (*continued page 8*)

Design Basics: Picking Out Your First Kayak

So you're thinking about getting a kayak? Looking at some of the fundamentals of kayak design will give you some perspective on what different shapes of kayaks will and won't do. Kayak design is a series of compromises; no single design does all things for all paddlers or even most things for an individual paddler.

First and fundamentally, a kayak, like a canoe and other slow-moving craft, is a displacement hull. To stay afloat and move through the water, it must displace a volume (weight) of water equal to the weight of the kayak, its passenger, and cargo. (Yes, kayaks can plane or surf under certain conditions, but that is a small portion of the time for most applications.) This below-waterline volume can be stretched into any number of shapes, long or short, wide or narrow, shallow or deep, but the volume must remain roughly constant. A kayak's length, width, depth, surface area, and volume are important components of the equation.

Length. A longer craft can be made narrower and have less draft, or depth in the water. Longer kayaks generally track better in a straight line and are faster than shorter, wider kayaks, whereas shorter kayaks turn, or maneuver, more quickly. A related characteristic is the *rocker*, the lengthwise curvature of the hull. A kayak with a straight keel line, which means it has little rocker, tracks very efficiently and resists turning, whereas one with lots of rocker has a greater depth, less waterline length, and pivots more easily.

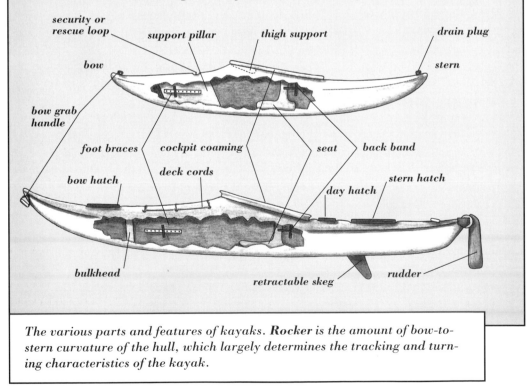

The various parts and features of kayaks. **Rocker** *is the amount of bow-to-stern curvature of the hull, which largely determines the tracking and turning characteristics of the kayak.*

Design Basics: Picking Out Your First Kayak

Width. The width in very general terms influences the stability of the kayak: wider boats are more stable. More specifically, the cross-sectional shape of the hull at its widest point indicates this stability or lack of it. A wide, flat bottom provides lots of stability—initial stability—in calm water, and a more rounded profile moves through the water more efficiently and is easier to lean into a turn. Flared sides above the waterline provide secondary, or reserve, stability as the kayak is leaned or rides over a wave.

Depth. More rocker as described in the Length section gives a kayak more depth in the center and makes it easier to turn but makes it relatively slower. A displacement hull has to have some depth, and a kayak that is too wide and long for the paddler and cargo has little depth, so it will slide off waves and blow around in the wind too easily.

Surface area. The wetted surface area of the hull—the shape that provides the displacement—creates drag while the kayak moves through the water, and designs that minimize this area are more efficient at forward motion. Wide, flat bottoms and hard chines—or edges—can add to this surface area. Many other factors, however, influence the overall efficiency of the hull; a spherical shape provides the least surface area but obviously has few other desirable characteristics.

Volume. The total volume of the kayak, both below and above the waterline, is important for a number of reasons. This volume must provide enough buoyancy for the intended type of kayaking in any big waves and rough seas, with larger kayaks providing a drier ride and more flotation. A certain amount of volume in the cockpit area must be for entering, sitting in the optimum position, and exiting. The volume, or shape, of the bow and stern sections above the waterline determines how the kayak handles in a variety of hydraulics and wind conditions.

Given the broad spectrum of kayaking activities, it is clear that the importance of each of these design characteristics varies with the type of kayaking being done. A closer look at usage categories pinpoints what some design aspects can do. (*continued next page*)

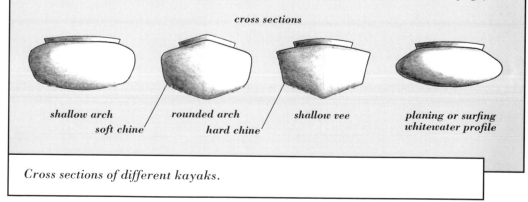

cross sections

shallow arch
soft chine

rounded arch
hard chine

shallow vee

planing or surfing
whitewater profile

Cross sections of different kayaks.

Design Basics: Picking Out Your First Kayak

(continued from previous page)

Whitewater

In the earlier days of the sport of whitewater kayaking—the days when I got started—the objective was merely to run the river successfully, negotiating the waves, drops, and eddies to the take-out point. The kayaks could be characterized as either slalom or downriver, with high to low volume variations. With the introduction of molded plastic kayaks, the appeal of the sport widened considerably, pushing the boundaries of the sport into many new variations.

Creek boating, squirt boating, rodeo acrobatics, and wave surfing have developed into major playboating niches, each with their specific designs that are evolving rapidly. Hot designs one season are likely to be old hat the next. Thus, prospective boat customers should develop their skills as much as possible first to understand better what aspect of whitewater matches their needs. Whitewater kayaking in any of its forms is a sport not only of personal skill and excitement, but also of cooperation, group safety, and appreciation of our river resources.

With most whitewater designs, ease of tracking is sacrificed for maneuverability, and with lengths down under 8 feet (2.4 m) on some models, the latest playboats are pretty sluggish in flatwater. Relatively flat bottoms enhance the ability of these kayaks to surf, and although widths need to be in the 24- to 27-inch range (61 to 69 cm) to provide adequate buoyancy, hard chines provide for precision control in complex water patterns. Low volume, spooned, and shaped bow and stern designs allow for submerged acrobatic stunts, whereas larger, fuller volumes are needed for drops, waterfalls, and big water conditions. Traditional slalom and wildwater designs have changed much less since the days of the 13-foot, 2-in. (4 m) standard.

Touring

Kayak designs that once were state-of-the-art whitewater or wildwater designs are now often used for entry-level paddling, general river touring, and even wilderness river running, where volume is needed for gear storage. Many new designs from the polyethylene-kayak manufacturers are oriented toward the growing recreational market of new paddlers who want forgiving craft for family use, exercise, fishing, and other pursuits on lakes, nontechnical rivers, and protected shorelines. This "touring" category is sort of a catch-all for a variety of kayak designs, including inexpensive polyethylene models, some folding kayaks, inflatables, and sit-on-tops.

Ease of handling and trackability are more important concerns in this category, and kayaks in the 12- to 15-foot (3.7 to 4.6 m) range with little to moderate rocker are

Design Basics: Picking Out Your First Kayak

the norm. Day-tripping doubles or larger, open-cockpit models to carry the kid or dog are available in the 14- to 17-foot (4.3 to 5.2 m) range. Stability for the majority of paddlers is also important, and widths from 24 to 30 inches (61 to 76 cm), with flat or shallow arched bottoms and forgiving soft chines, are the most typical. The volume in these touring kayaks is usually sufficient for hauling extra gear or for the occasional overnight.

Sea Kayaking

Once an esoteric sport found in just a few corners of the world, sea kayaking has become a mainstream recreational activity. Most other kayak designs can trace their roots back to European river kayaks, but most serious seaworthy kayak designs hark back in some form to the original Inuit kayaks of the Arctic regions. Serious sea kayaking, like serious whitewater paddling, is a sport of commitment, requiring a range of skills including paddling technique, seamanship, personal judgement, and environmental stewardship.

Sea kayaking implies going places, so these kayak designs are maximized for tracking efficiency without giving up seaworthiness. Models in the 16- to 17-foot (4.9 to 5.2 m) range generally track well while retaining some maneuverability in waves and surf. The 18- to 19-footers (5.5 to 5.8 m) are most at home carrying good-sized loads and covering lots of distance. Seaworthy tandem sea kayaks fall into the 19- to 22-foot range (5.8 to 6.7 m). Width-wise, 23 to 25 inches (58 to 63 cm) provide plenty of initial stability and room for larger paddlers, and the 19- to 22-inch (48 to 56 cm) beams sacrifice some of that initial stability for forward efficiency and rough-water responsiveness.

"Bluewater" paddling isn't necessarily flatwater paddling, so other characteristics are built into good sea kayaks so they can handle the unpredictable conditions of the sea. Deck surface area and cockpit position are configured to provide a balance in crosswinds and prevent excessive weathercocking. A bit of flare and upsweep to the bow reduce plunging into oncoming waves and give a drier ride. A straight keel line at the stern, or the use of a skeg or rudder, can improve tracking in certain conditions.

When shopping for any kayak, the choice of hull materials will have a major impact on the cost. Remember to budget for a good paddle, a spray skirt, PFD, and flotation. Polyethylene-hull kayaks are popular due to their moderate price ranges and are the material of choice for the rigors of whitewater paddling. Composite kayaks—fiberglass and other cloth laminates—offer weight savings and a more sophisticated array of designs, but at a greater price. Folding kayaks and inflatables offer a great degree of portability and ease of storage for those who travel. Wood-laminate *(continued next page)*

Design Basics: Picking Out Your First Kayak

(*continued from previous page*) and skin-on-frame kayaks are an alternative for those seeking the satisfaction of building or wishing to connect with more traditional designs.

You should consider the "investment" value of kayaking if you're concerned about the cost of the sport. First, most kayaks retain a reasonable resale value over time. And if you divide the cost of the boat by the number of years of enjoyable paddling, the cost per year becomes a very reasonable investment. You'll make a strong investment in your quality of life and a commitment toward a more environmentally friendly lifestyle.

Still, the most important thing you can do to learn is to get out there and try it. Take in some demos and other paddle events, try some instructional classes or guided tours, rent some kayak models if possible, and develop a sense of what will work for you, and what aspects of the spectrum of kayaking match your interests. Much of any decision will revolve around subjective considerations; after all, this is supposed to be fun. You can always trade up later, so make your best judgment and get out there and enjoy it.

(*continued from page 3*) take extra risks. Next is the competitive segment of the whitewater world in which highly specialized kayak designs are used for slalom, down river, and rodeo competition. Requiring highly refined skills, kayakers in this active niche may compete in events ranging from local club meets to the Olympics.

The majority of whitewater paddling is *recreational playboating,* a segment that has grown steadily since the introduction of polyethylene kayaks. Shorter and ever more stunt-oriented kayak designs reflect a sport in which kayakers no longer merely run the rivers but use whitewater as a liquid gymnasium for playful maneuvering and creating new lines of descent. A successful combination of adrenaline, competition, and cooperation within the group promotes personal advancement within a framework of river safety.

A fast-growing segment of *recreational touring* forms a broad middle band of the kayak spectrum. Somewhat longer and suited to going places on nontechnical rivers, lakes, and relatively protected shorelines, these kayaks fall into two classes: *classic* and *contemporary*. Older, traditional whitewater designs are being reinvented as river-touring and river-expedition boats for those who want to explore and sightsee more than to battle the rapids. Newer, contemporary kayaks, on the other hand, that are wide and stable and employ a relatively inexpensive polyethylene-hull construction, are being used for casual touring, day tripping, and family fun. Easy to paddle, these boats include solo and short tandem models, sit-on-top designs, and even inflatable models. Rentals and public paddlesport demos, which tend to use these newer designs, have introduced kayaking to a wide range of people.

Some of these recreational touring kayaks appeal to paddlers with a focused, goal-oriented mind-set. Usually a bit longer yet in length, these touring models efficiently cruise through miles of water and are used for exercise, overnight touring, exploration of protected waters, and perhaps fishing and photography. These kayaks are as likely to be used for solo paddling as for group outings.

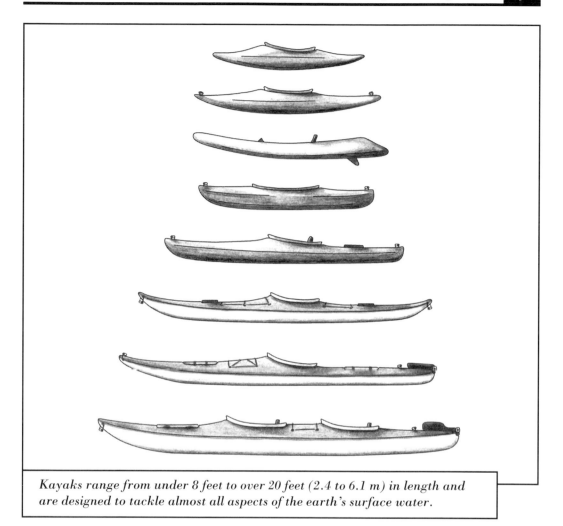

Kayaks range from under 8 feet to over 20 feet (2.4 to 6.1 m) in length and are designed to tackle almost all aspects of the earth's surface water.

Kayaks made for the open waters of big lakes and salt-water coastlines are longer still. Commonly called *sea kayaks* or *blue-water kayaks*, these craft are made to handle combinations of waves, wind, and weather that may be encountered beyond reach of protected shores, and require skills and judgment that take time to acquire. Sea kayakers usually share an appreciation for the natural environment, the joy of human-powered motion, and the satisfaction of successfully coping with a coastal water world. Variations on the sport of sea kayaking include races and skills competitions at organized events for those enthusiasts with a competitive streak. Quite often, this type of sea kayaker will find it natural to cross over to other water-based activities such as sailing or canoeing.

At the other end of the kayak spectrum, the cutting edge of paddlesports asserts itself in various frontiers. White-knuckle *ocean playboating* is on the increase in the surf zone and in extreme tidal conditions, utilizing specialized surf kayaks, whitewater playboats, as well as sea kayaks. Another variation of this sport, long-distance expedition sea kayaking, has explored the awesome unknowns of the oceans many times throughout the twentieth century.

Clearly, the world of kayaking is in reality a collection of different sports, driven by many different motivations. These different classes of kayaks will be discussed in more detail when we explore the theme of choosing a kayak and then outfitting and accessorizing it to your personal needs. If you find an interest in more than one aspect of the spectrum of kayaking, one boat may not be able to do everything you want, nor match your needs as your skills develop. Joining the club of multiple boat owners is a threshold to cross as you entertain a greater level of skills and commitment to what can become a lifelong avocation. You really didn't want to be able to get your car in the garage, did you?

The Future

As a form of recreational activity, paddlesports are not likely to disappear soon. Venerable names like Old Town and Klepper, around since 1898 and 1907, respectively, can attest to that. It would be premature to claim that the fundamentals of kayak design and human endurance are cast in stone. Equipped with advanced materials and an imaginative and adventurous human spirit, people will continue to explore new frontiers. What future directions will kayaking take? As rising populations gain affluence, putting greater pressures on scarce world resources, paddling-based activities will undoubtedly increase, providing a relatively inexpensive form of recreation with a low impact on the environment.

Many paddlers ask why anyone should promote paddlesports at all. There are already too many people on the rivers, at the launch sites, and in the camping areas, the reasoning goes. We all hate to see our secret places get discovered, but I think it's necessary to look at the issue with a wider perspective. Kayaking has provided many participants a realistic level of awareness of our place in nature and has fostered a sense of stewardship for the natural environment.

Drawing newcomers into the exciting world of paddlesports builds a constituency for the protection of water resources and the appreciation and preservation of our wild and natural areas. A growing paddlesports community, properly educated, will have an increasingly powerful voice concerning issues such as access, development, and pollution. Yes, your favorite surfing spots may be a bit more crowded and those secluded beaches may have a few more footprints, but an environmentally sensitive paddlesports community improves the chances that there will continue to be a water heritage for future generations to enjoy.

Finding Your Place

The myriad elements of the kayaking world take widely different directions and require different skills and motivations. Magazine articles, flashy videos, and enthusiastic stories of friends may make all of it sound exciting, but unless you have unlimited time and resources, you will need to focus on the aspect of kayaking that best suits your character. Any newcomer—perhaps having paddled awhile—should reassess his or her commitment to the sport. It pays to reflect about your strengths, skills, and goals, as well as to consider your available resources and your motivations, before deciding where you want to be on the kayaking "continuum." Consider, for example, the following reasons for taking up the sport of kayaking.

- Are you an A-type or a B-type paddler? Some kayakers are driven by the thrill of accomplishment, the adrenaline rush of approaching the edge of danger, and the stimulation of competition. Others are more influenced by such "quiet" values as an appreciation of the outdoors, the joy of pure exercise, or the peripheral goals of photography and fishing. These aspects occur in varying degrees in every segment of kayaking just as they naturally occur in other outdoor pursuits.

- Are you taking up kayaking to meet new people and be part of a group or are you looking for an avenue of water for solo relaxation and personal time out? All aspects of kayaking are conducive to paddling with others, and paddling in a coordinated group is the foundation of paddling safety. Recreational kayaking and kayak touring, however, are also conducive to solo excursions for those who sometimes want to "get away from it all."

- Is your goal one of expanding your physical skills, getting some serious exercise, and perhaps being competitive, or are you looking for a form of relaxation and escape from schedules and pressures? Kayaking can be a great form of serious training, and it can be one of the most satisfying forms of leisurely escapism. Your performance partly depends on your physical skills and abilities.

- Do you foresee committing all your leisure time and energy to the sport of kayaking, or will you be sharing your interest in kayaking with other outdoor sports, leisure activities, and family? Setting a realistic budget of time and money to devote to the sport can help you judge your level of commitment.

Kayakers can be motivated by many of these aspects of the sport. Kayaking and paddlesports can become a lifelong passion that will grow with you as an individual. At its more serious levels, it's a sport of commitment, and if you make that commitment, you can then look at your time and money as an investment rather than as an expense.

Kayaking as a Risk-Taking Activity

A few words of caution: kayaking, like any outdoor pursuit, involves a degree of risk, just as does anything else in our lives. Each day we make any number of decisions involving risk with some general understanding of the dangers involved, whether it be with automobiles, airplanes, high-fat foods, or midnight visits to a convenience store. This is the reality of our lives, just as it was for our ancient ancestors who had to come out of the cave and move on to the next valley.

One of kayaking's important skills you want to acquire from the outset is the ability to assess the risks involved as you progress to new levels of performance and exposure to potential hazards. Such judgment will come from a combination of raw experience, organized learning situations, communication with peers, and reference to the literature of the sport. We all have different tolerances as to our levels of acceptable risk, whether it be toward the cutting edge or the cautious, and by being able to judge the risks inherent in paddlesports, we can stay within our personal boundaries of safety. If you make use of the many opportunities in the sport for paddling education and interaction with others, you will be a safer, better paddler.

2
CHOOSING AND USING A KAYAK

In the enthusiasm of any new endeavor, especially when choosing the necessary equipment and getting it to work for you, it's all too easy to rush in headfirst and make expensive mistakes right out of the starting block. This book's central premise is to guide prospective kayakers as to which equipment will meet their needs, and then to explain how to keep this gear working in top-notch condition. Before rushing out with checkbook in hand, consider for a moment your options. Alternative approaches can lead to a wise and satisfying investment of your time and money. In reality, once you've been bitten by the kayaking bug, the purchase of a kayak should be well down the list of things to do first.

Try Before You Buy

Before making any major purchase, before signing the papers, you should take a test drive or do a thorough inspection—the same is true of kayaks. Remember that you're not just buying a boat and accessories; you're buying into a whole new lifestyle that should match your individual personality and goals.

Time is your best initial investment in the sport. Take the time to try your chosen version of kayaking in different conditions to be sure it meshes with your initial gut feeling. Sample the sport through guided trips, lessons, club activities, store demos and rentals, regional symposiums, and competitive events. Well-organized lesson programs and guided trips can quickly and safely introduce you to kayaking and the necessary skills that should be learned properly. Hundreds of paddling clubs in North America and other parts of the world cover whitewater to sea kayaking and typically most are happy to work with newcomers. You can rent equipment from various sources to get outfitted for these organized outings or to provide an alternate way to give paddling a try. Always seek advice, however, before venturing beyond your initial abilities.

Commercial and semi-commercial events—boat demos, expos, and symposiums—can also provide some initial experience and valuable contacts. But approach these events with a predetermined game plan. Don't allow yourself to get too wrapped up in the excitement and hype

The many kayak events—demos, races, rodeos, symposiums, and clinics— are great opportunities to learn more, meet fellow paddlers, and perhaps explore extraordinary waterways.

generated by the event. Perhaps you should leave your checkbook at home to allow for a cooling-off period and time to think about what you really need (my friends in the kayak industry won't be happy with that statement, though). When shopping for a specific kayak, many of these events can be used to test-paddle a particular boat. However, a ten-minute paddle may not give you enough information to make a good decision. To the extent possible, try the kayak in conditions approximating those in which you will most likely use it.

Finally, don't overlook learning as much as you can from other community resources such as libraries, clubs, Internet sources, local paddling shops, magazines, and books.

Where to Shop

You should consider a number of sources when shopping for a kayak and accessories. As with any other commodity, it's possible to acquire used boats, discounted bargains, as well as the latest in models from full-service dealers. With any of these options, the more you know about your own needs, the better your decision will likely be.

As you continue searching for more information and advice, become acquainted with local or regional specialty paddlesports stores or outdoor equipment stores with a strong paddlesports department. You're likely to find not just knowledgeable help in such environments but also other paddlers who can assist with your needs. A specialized activity such as kayaking requires skills and judgments that take time to learn. Look for an operation that provides more than the initial sale; a desirable paddlesports store can provide accessory selections, skills classes, on-water demos, support of local clubs, and contributions to conservation causes. The growth of the sport is a two-way street: by supporting the people associated with your local shop, they in turn can support the kayaking community.

You can get a good buy if you're willing to wait for the right deal. In general, the used-kayaks market is an active one in most areas. Check the bulletin boards of outdoor stores, club newsletters, and the classifieds of major-city newspapers to track down available boats. Assess the maintenance that may be needed on a potential purchase. (Use the information discussed later in this book.) Many paddlesports stores, rental outfitters, and guide services will sell off their rental and demo kayaks at certain predetermined times, allowing for some good values on well-worn but serviceable boats. Finally, if you're especially patient, follow the annual retail cycle in your area and watch for seasonal promotions and sales that may provide deals on the products you want. Some retailers may be willing to give a buying incentive if you special-order a kayak to be included with a seasonal shipment.

Although you can mail-order a kayak, shipping items of this size can be problematic. Freight surcharges, damage done by common carriers, and little recourse in the event of a warranty claim are some of the "hidden expenses." The reputation of the mail-order company is paramount when doing business this way. Try making a minor purchase from the prospective vendor to test their customer service before committing a grand or two to this method of buying.

The cheapest deal is only a good deal if the kayak suits your paddling needs. Think of your purchase as an investment; even if you need to invest a bit more to get what you need, chances are you can recoup a good portion of the original price if you ever resell. And don't forget that you're investing in some important intangibles: the enjoyment, the personal satisfaction, and the performance and safety that come with your choice.

Building a Kayak

One other option is to make a kayak yourself. This increasingly popular approach applies primarily to touring kayaks and sea kayaks. Relatively simple *stitch-and-glue plywood kayaks* are available in kit form and require minimal prior skills other than patience. *Wood strip* or *strip-built kayaks* and traditional *skin-on-frame designs* take a greater array of woodworking skills and a larger commitment in time. Building your own kayak saves a good chunk of money, unless you account for the time invested.

Choosing a Manufactured Kayak

We have discussed the various segments of the kayaking world in general terms. Once you have chosen a particular type of kayak, it's time to start narrowing down the choices. You should factor in the following considerations before making your final decision:

- **Price and budget.** Kayaking-wise, the initial investment is the big one; you've got to have a boat. As previously discussed, because kayaks usually have a reasonable resale value, don't be "penny-wise and pound-foolish." Consider the potential return on your investment through resale as part of your paddling budget. Kayaks made from *machine-molded polyethylene hulls* will cost less, and *composite kayaks*—hand-laid-up fiberglass, Kevlar or other reinforcing cloth bonded with a resin—will cost more, perhaps 50 to 100 percent more. Kayak accessories, such as the type of seat, foot braces, bulkheads, deck accessories, and rudders, some of which are necessary of course, will add to the price as well. Be realistic when adding accessories to your initial purchase; if you're the type of person who will probably never go on an expedition, don't buy the "expedition package." However, do factor into your budget the essentials—such accessories as a paddle, PFD (personal flotation device), spray skirt, flotation, helmet, and other items.

- **Performance.** There are books about kayak design, how they perform in the water, and the skills necessary to make them work. The point is do your research, assess your skills and motivations, and try to match yourself with an appropriate model. If you expect your skills to improve and your commitment to the sport to increase, choose a kayak that you can "grow into," a kayak that accommodates both your current abilities and future needs. It's important to be able to cope with the kayak initially. But you will only be a beginner for a short period of time, and some of the higher performance niches of kayaking will require progressing through a few design stages. The fit of your kayak is equally important for performance and control on the water. Your body size and shape may dictate the type of cockpit and size of kayak necessary for your needs.

- **Weight.** If you anticipate trouble getting your kayak on and off a vehicle, consider its weight. *Polyethylene kayaks* are generally heavier than *composite kayaks* or *wood kayaks*. If you plan to enter competitive kayaking events, again consider the kayak's weight. Built for situations in which every ounce counts, exotic composite-hull kayaks give racers an edge. This type of kayak is the choice for racing and other competitive forms of kayaking.

- **Personal preferences.** A number of personal biases will influence the choice of kayak, and you're perfectly within your rights to heed them. Comfort, style, color, and other subjective features can influence your enjoyment of a particular model. Besides, this is all supposed to be fun anyway.

Next, let's look at some additional options within the various branches of kayaking. You can turn to a number of sources for further information on specific models. For a start, the annual Buyer's Guide issue of *Canoe & Kayak* gives a rundown of all the known kayaks on the market, including basic specifications. You can also obtain catalogs and additional information from the individual manufacturers or their local dealers in your area.

Whitewater Kayaks

Regional differences in the recreational whitewater scene are due in part to the differing size and nature of rivers, the popularity of certain brands of kayaks, and the influence of local paddling clubs and competitive events. When shopping for a whitewater kayak, seek the advice of influential paddlers in your paddling area and then choose a boat that will mesh well with your skills and allow you to keep pace with your circle of paddling friends.

As the variety of skills that loosely fit into the realm of whitewater playboating get refined, redefined, and reinvented, one breed of kayaks in response to these new skills has gotten shorter, more maneuverable, and more focused on certain techniques. The hot kayak designs of a few years back have become today's entry-level models and tomorrow's old beaters and loaners. For years the standard whitewater kayak length was 13 feet, 2 inches (4 m), and now some models are less than 8 feet (2.4 m). Quickening the pace of change, some manufacturers are introducing new models more than once a year. Therefore a bargain on the market may only be a bargain if you know exactly what the particular model will be able to do for you and it matches what you want to accomplish with your paddling time.

Currently, the hottest whitewater kayaks are the short models, running from under 8 to about 10 feet (2.4 to 3 m) in length, which cost from $800 to $1,000 in polyethylene. A relatively small market exists for *performance composite whitewater kayaks*, which cost up to 50 percent more.

Whitewater kayaks longer than 10 or 12 feet (3 to 3.7 m) tend to be used now by larger paddlers, for handling bigger-volume rivers, or for general whitewater river touring. Dagger and Perception are the North American market-share leaders, with Prijon of Germany, Wave Sport, Pyranha of England, Savage, Riot of Canada, and others providing stiff competition.

Recreational Kayaks

Stability and user friendliness are often the prime design features of this category of kayak. If shopping for a kayak that a number of people will use, such as one to be kept at a summer lake home, look for one that is easy to get in and out of, with easily adjustable seat and foot controls, and offering relatively good tracking characteristics for the first-timer. Kayaks with two seats for either tandem or solo paddling are often ideal for communal use. In places with warm water and easy but regular surf, short recreational kayaks and *sit-on-tops* may also be ideal for this kind of recreational use. Rock-solid stability may be desired for specialized uses such as fishing, hunting, and photography.

Virtually all kayaks in this particular category will be made of molded polyethylene and will cost between $350 and $750 new, depending on options. Kayak length will range from about 10 to 14 feet (3 to 4.3 m) and weight from 40 to 60 pounds (18 to 27 kg). Leading manufacturers of recreational kayaks include Old Town, Dagger, Perception, Wilderness Systems, Necky Kayaks, and Walden.

For the more serious paddler who wants to cover some distance and explore a backwater or get a good workout, kayaks in the 12- to 15-foot (3.7 to 4.6 m) range will generally *track* better in a straight line and *cruise* more efficiently, while offering *stability* and moderate price ranges. For those wanting to save as much weight as possible, composite kayaks are available in this niche. Don't overlook the importance of enough *flotation* in a kayak; many kayaks in this class have inadequate flotation built into them and should have additional *float bags* put in place.

Touring and Sea Kayaks

Continuing down the pyramid, one finds longer kayaks designed for more committed touring—daylong to weekend tours on nontechnical rivers, lakes, and relatively protected coastal zones.

These kayaks will be 14 to 16 feet (4.3 to 8.9 m) long and will usually have such built-in features as bulkheads and storage compartments, adjustable seats, and perhaps a rudder system. This class of *polyethylene-hull* touring kayak will weigh around 45 to 65 pounds (20 to 29 kg) and price out at $600 to $1,200 or so. A *composite-hull* alternative will reduce overall weight by about 10 pounds (4.5 kg) but will cost about $200 to $500 more than the polyethylene model. A number of wooden kayaks in this category are available in kit or finished form and provide additional weight savings and pride of ownership.

Differences between *touring* and *sea kayaks* are a matter of degree—features being added and design parameters enhanced for performance in open-water conditions. Therefore, it's important when shopping for a touring kayak to have a clear idea of the kinds of paddling conditions you might encounter. Whereas a full-blown sea kayak may be quite serviceable for casual inland paddling, don't assume that you can rely on a shorter, less expensive, touring kayak out on the open seas. When the going gets rough, the short kayak could be dangerously deficient in its ability to head where you want it to.

Most real sea kayaks fall into the 16- to 18-plus-foot (4.9 to 5.5 m) range for a single, with some combination of *deck profile* and *cockpit placement* to provide a minimum of *weathercocking* in cross winds. Also characteristic, a degree of *upsweep* in the kayak bow allows it to ride up and over oncoming waves; how much upsweep is necessary is debatable. Additional costly accessorizing, such as *bulkheads*, *skegs*, pumps, and *deck grab lines*, though typical, may not be needed for inland or river touring. Prices for polyethylene sea kayaks range from about $900 to $1,500, and in composites from $1,500 to almost $3,000.

Sea kayaks offer the greatest variation in width, ranging from 19 to over 25 inches (48 to +63 cm) or more for a single. In general, the wider the kayak, the greater its stability. Kayak width also determines the amount of *initial,* or *calm water,* stability and to some extent the load capacity of the boat, with a wider kayak providing more. These advantages, however, nibble at the kayak's efficiency because as it moves through water, a wider boat requires more energy to part the water around its hull. Perhaps the most commonly debated facet of sea kayak design, the stability versus efficiency trade-off, will most likely be the focal point of your search for the perfect boat. There are other important considerations in the choice of a sea kayak, of course, and we will be hitting on many of these distinctions throughout the book.

Double sea kayaks—models with two or more passenger cockpits—are popular in some areas, particularly in the Pacific Northwest. These large boats range from about 16 to 22 feet (4.9 to 6.7 m) and are more expensive, adding up to over $3,500 in some cases. Serious *tripping doubles* demand length—at least 19 feet (5.8 m)—to provide the efficiency and cargo storage capacity necessary for longer tours. Extensive travel in a tandem kayak requires a degree of synchronized paddling to be most efficient, as well as a shared temperament as to pace, routes, and so on; otherwise, a pair of single kayaks will more effectively keep the peace.

The sea kayak market presents an astonishing selection of brands and models, perhaps greater than almost any other category of merchandise. This surfeit of kayaks may be due to the continued popularity of composites and wood as hull materials of choice, which do not require a large capital investment to produce, allowing many small manufacturers with a passion for the sport to compete in the marketplace. This sea of kayaks can be confusing to the prospective buyer. While looking over the choices, be patient and consider some of these smaller suppliers. However, try not to get bogged down in the meantime; after all, you want to get out paddling, and any number of these choices will probably work just fine.

The polyethylene brands most popular in North America include Perception, Dagger, Necky, Wilderness Systems, and Prijon; the composite brands include Current Designs, Dagger, Necky, Wilderness Systems, Seda, Eddyline, Northwest Kayaks, Pacific Water Sports, Seaward, Mariner, Easy Rider, Valley Canoe Products, P & H Designs, and Nigel Dennis Kayaks, among others. My apologies to those I've missed.

Specialized Kayaks

Several categories of kayaks, having features designed for specialized situations, defy being pigeonholed into the groupings discussed so far.

Folding kayaks hark back to the original construction method used by Inuits—the *skin-on-frame* configuration. Easily collapsible and packable, this variation enabled early recreational users to transport their kayaks before the advent of the automobile. Today's durable synthetics like Hypalon have largely replaced the original canvas skins, and the folding frames can be aluminum alloy as well as wood, but the ease of transport and storage remain the appeal of these venerable kayaks. Design specifications for folding kayaks require a precision and complexity reflected in prices from almost $2,000 to over $4,000. Klepper, Feathercraft, Nautiraid, Folbot, and Seavivor are the major players in this market.

Inflatable kayaks, thanks to improved materials and designs, are becoming more serious contenders. Like folding kayaks, simple storage and manageable transportation, coupled with

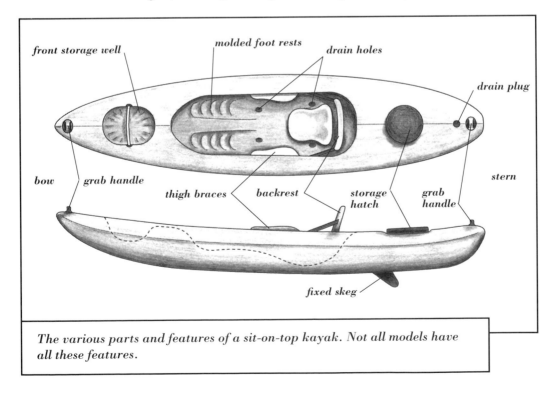

The various parts and features of a sit-on-top kayak. Not all models have all these features.

moderate price points and ease of use, make inflatables attractive to the entry-level or casual user. Lack of control in windy conditions and a relative lack of cargo space make them most suited for day tripping on rivers or in protected waters. The least expensive inflatables tend to be little more than beach toys, but as you move up the price scale, models will be made from more durable materials and utilize sophisticated designs. Top-end inflatables can be quite serviceable for white-water fun and rugged conditions. Models from such manufacturers as A.I.R.E., Grabner, Sevylor, and others will cost from $200 to $1,600 or so.

A relatively new type of paddlecraft, considered a kayak by some due to its use of a double-bladed paddle, is the *sit-on-top* (SOT). Some purists debate if these are really kayaks at all since they lack an enclosed deck, but leaving semantics aside, we will include them in the present discussions. The retail distribution and the intended use of the sit-on-tops tend to parallel that of traditional kayaks and provide an alternative craft useful in some situations, although they are unlikely to replace the role of decked craft in most serious paddling situations.

The primary advantage of the SOT format is the ease of entry and reentry in the water, resulting in the often-promoted feature of "no rolling." In reality, *rolling* and *bracing* are essential skills that build confidence and are part of the natural domain for any serious whitewater, open water, and surf paddling. A sit-on-top must be rigged up with seat and thigh brace systems to allow for these techniques if paddling in any rough water conditions is likely. Other applications, however, such as fishing, snorkeling, and just messing around on the water are ideal on a sit-on-top.

Because the encompassing deck of traditional kayaks protects paddlers from the elements, especially in cold water and severe weather conditions, SOTs are limited to the summer months and to the more southern latitudes. As with other recreational kayaks, SOT designs range from casual summer-home lake models to serious cruising and surfing craft. Most of these SOT models are made of polyethylene and cost from $300 to $900. Ocean Kayak, Old Town, Wilderness Systems, Perception, and Dagger have the lion's share of this market, with Heritage Kayaks and Island Kayaks providing new alternatives.

Choosing the Proper Accessories

You should put as much thought and research into the accessories as you do into the kayak of your choice. It doesn't make much sense, for example, to get the latest whitewater playboat design and then try to get by with a cheap nylon spray skirt that won't stay fastened down in heavy water. If on a rigid budget, plan out your key accessory purchases first, and then figure your kayak budget, or even consider renting a kayak for awhile until everything adds up. You will never regret the money invested in good paddles, PFDs, spray skirts, and flotation.

Paddles

Several kayak instructors I know like to emphasize that your choice of a paddle is more important than your choice of a boat. Whether or not this statement is entirely true, it points out the critical role the paddle plays in transforming human energy into forward motion. Many factors, which vary depending on the individual, can enter into the choice of a good paddle. Consider the following:

- **Weight.** Generally, the lighter the better, unless you're planning to fend off bears. You will be lifting the paddle over and over for hundreds of hours, and the energy saved with a lighter paddle adds up. Lighter paddles tend to cost more, so you may have to draw the line somewhere. Also, the lightest paddles are not the most durable, so if you're hard on your gear, go for a combination of strong-but-light paddle. Remember to consider the swing weight of the paddle. A paddle with a light shaft and heavy blades feels more sluggish than one with a heavier shaft and lighter blades. You can easily test this by "paddling air" while comparing paddles in a shop—just don't clobber anyone!

- **Style.** Paddle makers and models are as abundant as kayak manufacturers and models. Take your time shopping around, and test a variety of blade designs on the water if possible. Larger blades provide more power, acceleration, and leverage for bracing; medium or smaller blades are more comfortable to cruise with over time. Wood paddles are enjoying a resurgence in interest, especially the so-called Greenland or Inuit styles for touring, which require their own paddling technique. There will be a bit of a weight penalty with wood paddles, however. The standard wider-bladed paddles, sometimes referred to as European-style paddles, may have asymmetrically shaped blades to balance the torquing forces in the water, and they may have ovaled or bent-shaft handgrip areas to increase comfort and efficiency.

- **Length.** There is a trend toward shorter paddles in almost all forms of kayaking, coupled with a more focused, aggressive paddling style. The common range in whitewater paddling is 195 to 205 centimeters, 210 to 235 centimeters for touring. Take some lessons or observe the stroke techniques of some good paddlers before you decide on a certain length. Energetic paddling requires a shorter paddle than a more laid-back approach. Besides your paddling style, the width or *beam* of your boat will determine how much length will be needed to have the entire blade engaged in the water during the forward stroke.

- **Feathered versus unfeathered blade configuration.** This style of paddle blades is guaranteed to get a lively discussion going. Whether *unfeathered paddles*—both blades positioned on the shaft in the same plane—are easier on the wrists or whether *feathered-angle paddles* are better for bracing can be debated into the early hours. There has been a trend toward lower feather angles in recent years, 60 degrees and even 45 degrees instead of 90 or 75 degrees. Take some lessons, learn one way, and stick with it.

- **Take-apart paddles.** Two-piece paddles are easier to transport and are easier to store on deck as spares, a plus at least for touring kayaks. The good ones will have tight, reinforced *ferrules* so that durability should not be an issue. Three- and even four-piece paddles are available for storing as spares in cramped whitewater kayaks.

Spray Skirts

Your kayak spray skirt is an essential accessory. It keeps water out of the boat, especially in rough conditions, and should fit both you and the kayak comfortably with a minimum of loose fabric left over. Neoprene skirts usually fit best and are suitable for rolling, though the material doesn't "breathe," which can create discomfort in warm weather. A good nylon skirt, on the other hand, is cooler in warm weather and will be adequate for all but the most demanding situations. Hybrid neoprene-nylon skirts are a popular compromise. When buying a skirt, try it on so you can be sure to leave waist room for your paddling duds. Also bring your kayak along to assure a good, secure fit. For safety, a good skirt should have a grab loop that allows you to release the skirt from the cockpit coaming in the event of a wet exit.

Personal Flotation Devices

PFDs, life vests, buoyancy aids, or whatever you want to call them are your primary safety device while in the water. The key here is fit. Put as much time into shopping for a good fit in a PFD as you would for a good coat. Due to the recent explosion of different brands and styles, virtually anyone should be able to find a PFD with both a proper fit and some style.

3
KEEPING YOUR KAYAK IN TOP CONDITION

Like any piece of equipment, your boat is an investment. Of course, it's an investment in fun—you have chosen kayaking as a source of enjoyment and personal growth. But there can also be a substantial payback of additional service and resale value through proper care and maintenance. The bottom line of preventive maintenance is realizing a maximized resale value of major items, making it easier to trade up to new designs as your skills improve and as technology changes.

It can also be very satisfying whenever you extract the maximum useful life from a product and break the cycle of use-and-throw-away that is a part of today's consumer culture. A kayak and a paddle are not complex pieces of equipment. Their ageless simplicity not only adds to the mystique that can make kayaking a lifetime passion but also makes basic kayak care an easy task.

Basic Preventive Maintenance

The easiest form of maintenance takes place on the water. Extend the life of your boat and gear by not abusing them. Understanding that no kayak is meant for all seasons and conditions will dictate how hard you can be on it. Fiberglass sea kayaks, for example, are not intended for running technical whitewater rivers, and to do so is to invite trouble. No matter what they say, manufacturers have yet to make a kayak that can do it all.

If you intend to push the limits of your gear, shop with durability as your primary design criterion. Skills training will enable you to better judge hazards and to take appropriate avoidance measures. Also, the more experience on the water you have "under your paddle," the better your ability to plan trips that will not venture into foreseen difficulties.

Kayaks and other watercraft are unique in that they can travel over water for hundreds and even thousands of miles and be none the worse for it. Most of the wear and tear that requires maintenance comes from how boats are handled on land or during the launching and landing process. Serious damage can also occur in rough water conditions when the kayak is forced into obstructions, as on rivers or in the ocean surf.

The *shoreline zone*—the area where you depart from and return to the land—is where minor and occasionally major damage is most likely to occur. Babying your boat in this zone has a far greater impact on how long it lasts than does hard paddling once it's afloat. You can avoid or control much of the minor surface abrasion to the kayak hull by entering and exiting the kayak carefully. Conditions permitting, position your kayak so that it floats freely when you climb in, reducing abrasion from a sliding launch and avoiding the temptation of using your paddle as a pushing pole. This extra care is a trade-off, of course, taking a bit more time and resulting in wet feet. In wave or surf conditions you need to launch perpendicular to the wave patterns, and group members can help each other launch to cut down on the banging around that the kayaks get from the incoming waves.

When returning to shore, even though it may be tempting to ram your kayak as far up on the beach as possible, you pay a small price for each landing. Paddle into the shallows as close to shore as practical and step out, bracing with your paddle if necessary. If the water is cold and you want to keep your feet dry, invest in good footwear. When landing in surf, you will not have the luxury of a leisurely exit. The best you can do is to minimize awkward landings and get the kayak higher up the beach before the next wave of equal size. Be ready to exit the kayak quickly, avoid getting hit by it if waves push it around, and drag it above the waterline as soon as possible.

At times there will be opportunities to launch and land at docks, jetties, or other artificial structures. Although these provide easy access and reduce abrasion on the bottom of the boat, watch out for bolts or other sharp protrusions that can gouge the kayak's sides. Be especially cautious of strong currents, reflected waves, and other hazardous conditions.

To minimize serious boat damage, avoid difficult conditions in the first place. Do not enter into moving water, whether a technical whitewater river or an ocean surf zone, without a working knowledge of the forces involved, and such water is certainly not a place to paddle alone. Seek out professional instruction, put in hours of practice, and learn relevant rescue procedures if you want to be proficient and safe. Even if you don't intend to paddle in these conditions, having the necessary route-finding and water-reading skills will enable you to avoid venturing into dangerous situations.

Mistakes made in moving water can lead to traumatic damage to your kayak. Minimize this with the liberal use of flotation. As we discuss on page 103, all unused space in the cockpit should be filled with float bags or foam to displace the weight of water. If you come out of your boat, this displacement can mean the difference between a hundred-pound and a thousand-pound missile surging into a rock or crashing onto a beach. If you're on an extended trip, loaded kayaks may feel more stable in moving and turbulent water, but will be much less maneuverable, so think farther ahead as to what navigational situations are coming up and skip the tricky moves.

Avoiding Land-Based Wear and Tear

The other likely source of wear and tear on your kayak is during the transport phase—either while it's on a vehicle or when it's being moved to and from the launch site. However sleek they are on the water, kayaks are cumbersome hulks on the land. And it's when paddlecraft are out of their element that you will most appreciate the value of lightness. Transportation, hauling, and portaging (discussed in detail in chapter 7) present three common sources of boat damage. Dragging kayaks to and from the water, especially across hard surfaces like parking lots, is one way to damage your kayak. Overexuberant or poorly designed tie-down methods can cause cracking or deforming. Airborne kayaks—kayaks that have not been tied down properly to moving vehicles—can suffer catastrophic damage.

Avoid using your kayak and paddling equipment for non-paddling purposes. Kayaks are not designed to be picnic tables, beach chairs, or cutting boards. Paddles do not make good shovels or tent poles. And PFDs have more important duties than as ground cushions on gravelly beaches. You may have compelling reasons, but making your gear do double-duty on paddle tours can lead to surface scratches and possibly structural damage.

Hull Maintenance Considerations

The kayak hull materials available have varying properties from a maintenance standpoint. The following evaluation of these materials will help you understand how to keep your kayak seaworthy and also looking good.

The majority of kayaks are now made from molded polyethylene—a reasonably inexpensive material that also provides good impact resistance. Though not indestructible, polyethylene, because of its resilience, is the material of choice for most types of whitewater paddling, for rental operations, and for touring kayakers looking for ease of use. To perform in the water, most *poly* (polyethylene) *kayaks* are outfitted with a system of bulkheads or pillars, which helps to stiffen the kayak's profile. Durability doesn't mean maintenance-free, however. Polyethylene is a relatively soft material that is easily scratched and fuzzed up by repeated abrasion. It can be deformed by heat and excess pressure, although a *memory* characteristic to molded polyethylene helps it return to its manufactured shape. Most manufacturers add *UV inhibitors* to their mix to reduce ultraviolet radiation deterioration of the polyethylene hull. Nevertheless, the adverse effect of ultraviolet rays, which can be intensified on the water, needs to be considered. Whereas a polyethylene hull is not very likely to split or puncture, repairing such damage can be problematic.

Typical scratches and abrasion in the hull of a polyethylene whitewater kayak.

Composite kayaks, made with some combination of fiberglass, Kevlar, or carbon fiber, are stiffer and generally lighter than polyethylene, but they lack the same strength of poly to withstand traumatic impact. On all but the lightest composites, the outer gelcoat surface provides a hard, scratch-resistant barrier protecting the structural core. Scratches, worn spots, and more serious impact points that occur to composites usually can be repaired with relative ease.

Wood strip and *plywood kayaks* used for touring purposes are also reasonably durable when it comes to surface abrasion and general banging around, and repairs to these *lay-ups* are pretty straightforward. *Skin-on-frame* and *folding kayaks* are as durable as the skin material allows. *Coated canvas* and *synthetic skins* such as Hypalon can withstand quite a bit of shoreline abrasion but need to be protected from unusually sharp or pointed obstructions. The natural flexibility of these kayak frames provides some *give* so the skin doesn't take the full force of an impact.

Inflatable kayaks also provide a lot of cushioning from impacts, but like other flexible fabric hulls, they need to be protected from sharp obstructions. In a river or beach environment, this can include sharp, unnaturally shattered rocks, broken glass, submerged hazards such as metal posts, and broken branches of downed trees. In short, what you give up in durability, you need to make up with greater vigilance on the water.

Routine Maintenance

It's all too easy to throw your gear in a pile at the end of a paddle trip, forget about it, and then hurriedly scrape it all together again the next time you want to take your kayak out on the water. The first and perhaps hardest step toward proper maintenance of your equipment is to develop the habit of regularly looking things over, checking for problems and possible repair jobs by making a visual inspection—beginning with your kayak. A few extra moments spent before and after kayak outings can eliminate many problems. The end of a trip when your memory is fresh with the scrapes, bumps, and other mishaps of the day is a good time to look at, mark, or at least mentally note problems that warrant attention before the next trip. Set aside time for more thorough inspections before a major trip or at the beginning of the season.

Most routine kayak maintenance is fairly basic; you don't need magic formulas to keep things in tune, just an observant eye. Keeping your gear in good condition will give you the satisfaction and the confidence of knowing it won't let you down the next time you're out on the water. In this review, we will go over the parts of the kayak and do minor maintenance. Chapter 4 discusses repair work in more detail.

Giving Your Kayak a Check-Up

First, stay in tune with the integrity of your kayak's hull. Every time you load the kayak on your vehicle, you have an opportunity to do a quick visual check. Look along the keel line for signs of wear, gouges, or chipped gelcoat. *Hard chines*—angled lines between deck and hull of certain kayaks—may be wear points as well. The thinner sidewalls of a composite hull, roughly along the water line, may be susceptible to stress fractures from impacts both on and off the water. The sections of a hull adjacent to bulkheads, pillars, and seats, being stiffer from the interior support, may precipitate greater amounts of abrasion. If you know you hit something while paddling, check the suspected area of the hull more closely once out of the water.

Periodically during the season, turn the kayak upside-down, perhaps using a pair of sawhorses or sturdy benches to get a better working position, and look closely for problem spots. Use a bright flashlight or electric utility lamp to shine through the hull to get a clearer view of the extent and depth of a crack or gouge.

Surface damage to the deck of a kayak is rare and is more likely to be noticed when it happens. Chips and cracks along the edge of the cockpit coaming are less obvious. If irregular or sharp, these points can cause trouble for your spray skirt. Other sources of deck scratches can include impacts from errant paddle strokes and from items being slid in and out of the *deck bungee cords (bungees)*.

What should you do about all these scratches and nicks? First, determine which are cosmetic and which are structural and need more immediate attention. Obviously, any point of damage that leaks requires some sort of repair before the boat is used. Attend promptly to cracks and chips in composite hulls that leave the fabric under the gelcoat exposed or stress cracks that have weakened the stiffness of the hull. The dozens of shallow scratches, gouges, dings, or areas of abrasion that any hull will sustain add to the character of the kayak. You can tinker with these minor nicks at a later date.

Chapter 4 goes into more depth on repairing surface problems. As for basic maintenance and temporary repairs to keep you temporarily afloat, that trusty roll of duct tape is hard to beat. Small cracks, leaks, and areas of weakness can be protected with a strip or two of tape. If a crack is visible from the inside of the hull, put a piece of tape on that point as well to keep dirt out. Keep in mind that this is a temporary solution and that the affected spot should be protected from further impacts. Duct tape deteriorates relatively quickly in sunlight and water and should not be relied upon indefinitely. For safety's sake, avoid using a damaged kayak in extreme or remote conditions.

To smooth over the many minor hull scratches, consider applying a layer of automotive or marine wax. It's debatable whether this will add efficiency or "speed" to the hull, but your kayak will look newer and have a minor level of additional protection. Remember that you will need to clean off thoroughly any wax covering spots before patching them later.

Ultraviolet deterioration affects most hull materials. This gradual breakdown in the strength, resiliency, and color of many materials should not be a serious problem for the average recreational kayaker, unless the kayak is stored in a sunny location or the boat is used for many weeks out of the year. Polyethylene and fabric-hulled kayaks are the most susceptible, but keeping all boats, as well as accessories, out of the sun whenever possible is beneficial.

Gelcoat-surfaced composite kayaks, though structurally not weakened, will gradually fade, even taking on a white chalky look. Non-gelcoated clear Kevlar lay-ups, which can allow deterioration of the Kevlar itself, should be given additional care. Treat varnished or epoxied wood kayaks with a UV-resistant varnish or paint.

Use a UV inhibitor such as 303 Protectant or Armorall for UV protection of deck and hull areas. These products absorb the energy of the UV radiation, maintaining and even enhancing UV protection, and like wax on an auto body, they can protect the surface of the hull from atmospheric and waterborne pollutants. The coatings gradually break down and can be worn off by abrasion but can be reapplied once or twice a season without much effort.

Seams and Joints

On a wood, skin-on-frame, or composite kayak, the cockpit coaming is installed into the deck as a separate piece, and the resulting seam may be a weak point where damage can occur, sometimes from repeated sitting on the coaming while sliding into the seat. In a composite boat this seam can be either fiberglassed, which is the strongest method, or bonded with an adhesive sealant. Check for gaps, cracks, or leak points around this perimeter.

Composite-hull kayaks also have a seam between the hull and the deck where the two halves are manually joined or inserted into an *H-channel extrusion.* Check for any signs of separation or breaks in the extrusion. The inside of such a seam is usually fiberglassed together,

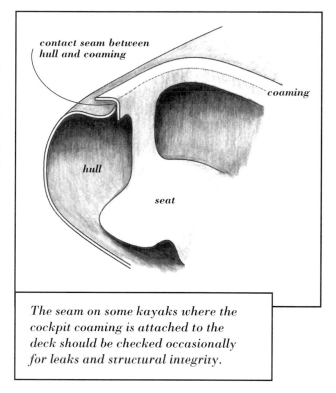

The seam on some kayaks where the cockpit coaming is attached to the deck should be checked occasionally for leaks and structural integrity.

which is the structural part of the seam. Leaking can occur if this tape is damaged; usually it takes a bit of an impact to do so.

If you suspect leaking along this side seam, or at any other point, do a water test to pinpoint the location of the leak. If water can find its way into the kayak, it will also be able to flow the opposite way. Prop up the kayak in such a way that the suspected leaky area faces downward and fill that area with water to determine where it's seeping through. This "leak technique" is not foolproof. It may take a bit of experimenting, on the water in some cases, to find the source of the leak. I once tinkered around off and on for about a year looking for a slow leak that turned out to be water pumped in by capillary action down the rudder cable channel while paddling on choppy wave days.

Also, remember that water is heavy; make certain the hull is adequately supported before loading it with more than a few gallons. For delicate skin-on-frame or ultralight composite kayaks, it may suffice to give the outside of the hull a blast of water from a garden hose and then check the seam or crack from the inside for signs of water. The skin material of a folding kayak can be inspected while the craft is disassembled. One approach is to hold seams and suspected areas of abrasion down in a laundry tub of water.

Maintenance of Components

Periodically inspect the less visible internal components of your kayak for potential problems. All kayaks have some sort of seat, and these arrangements can be as diverse as the number of models of boats on the market, ranging from simple foam blocks to complex adjustable seats mounted on tracks. Since you will be spending many hours sitting in the kayak, the seat arrangement is a prime candidate for customizing to your own needs (see chapter 5). As far as maintenance of your present setup goes, check to verify that components are securely fastened in place and that any adjustable parts are functioning.

Polyethylene-hull kayaks often have a generic *rotomolded seat* that comes with either a back band or a rigid seat back. Check this setup for proper adjustment, making sure that webbing, buckles, and/or knots are secure. The seat may also help hold a stiffening rod or bulkhead arrangement in place that needs to be kept secure for safety reasons. Clean sand and other debris out of the space between the seat unit and the bottom of the hull to prevent abrasion and wear points on the hull.

Composite kayaks often come with a hanging seat that is part of the cockpit coaming unit. Usually supported by sections of foam wedged underneath and on the sides, these seats also can accumulate sand and other stuff underneath them, which can create points of wear. If the seat has a hinged backrest, check the hinge points for wear. Bolts used as hinge points can wear away the surrounding fiberglass. Flexible plastic hinges may be more trouble-free, but check for any signs of cracking or loosening. These adjustable seat backs usually have a control line that ties off or runs through a *clam cleat*. Especially in fiberglass seats, this line may be susceptible to abrasion where it wraps around a sharp corner. Restore plastic cleats that have lost their "bite" over time by sharpening the teeth with a small file or folded piece of sandpaper.

Padded nylon webbing *back bands* are becoming more popular. Though generally trouble-free, you need to tweak the fit of these items periodically. Check the way they are mounted to the seat frame or the coaming and watch for wear of the nylon band and any stretch cord attachments.

On custom-built and folding kayaks, make sure the seat is securely attached and won't go merrily floating away in the event of a capsize. Sit-on-top kayaks rigged for serious paddling will have a thigh-strap system and perhaps a padded seat arrangement, which should be periodically fine-tuned for fit and security. Look at the integrity of attachment points to the hull. This is where they receive a good deal of stress.

If possible, remove and wash any nylon, fabric, and foam parts in fresh water to remove grime and dried salt residue. Modern plastic buckles and fasteners are pretty maintenance free, but try to keep sand out of them. For hard-to-reach fixtures inside the hull, try propping or hanging the kayak upside down at a comfortable standing height to facilitate working on those parts.

Creating a handy kayak workstand can be as simple as mounting your cartop kayak mounts to a pair of sawhorses or other sturdy bases. Try to arrange the height to minimize strain on your back.

Interior Kayak Parts

Foot braces, particularly adjustable ones, require maintenance. Adjustable foot braces are designed to accommodate paddlers of different leg lengths, as well as differing types of footwear. Because these braces usually slide back and forth in some sort of track, they are prone to clog with sand or small pebbles. Some have spaces drilled or cut into the track, which makes them somewhat self-cleaning. Especially if you rarely tinker with these settings, check them periodically to prevent them from seizing up. Fixed-position foot pegs or footrests are more trouble-free, particularly if they take the form of a bar, platform, or bulkhead. Just make sure they remain fixed in place. In a well-used kayak, your heels may over time create a worn spot in the hull where they are positioned, but it's more likely that your paddle shoes will wear out first. More importantly, as a safety precaution, make sure that any foot brace or footrest system doesn't trap your feet in such a way as to prevent an emergency exit.

Sliding foot pedals that are used to control rudder positions are also susceptible to clogging. If they cease moving freely, take them apart, clean out any trapped sand, and if necessary, apply a powdered graphite lubricant. Hint: avoid using liquid lubricants, which attract more dirt. While inspecting these pedals, also look at the condition of the cable or line that runs back to the rudder. Cable wear is unusual at the splice connecting it to the braces and is more likely at the point where it passes over an edge or through the hull.

Cables can be run to the stern and passed through the hull in several ways. Some methods use plastic tubing to run cables past the seat and any rear bulkhead or flotation obstructions. A more sophisticated method found in composite kayaks runs cables along the inside of a small channel built into the H seam that holds the hull and deck together. Although impossible to see what is going on inside the channels, if the cable is moving freely, it's probably not bent or frayed. If, however, the line or cable is exposed anywhere along its path, make sure that it does not get pinched by gear packed in tightly or that it isn't sawing its way through flotation or storage bags.

Bulkheads, Pillars, and Flotation

All kayaks should have a built-in system of pillars or bulkheads and/or flotation bags. These systems have two general purposes. One is to provide structural rigidity and safety to the hull. The other purpose is to provide adequate flotation and storage. Kayaks use various combinations of these structures depending on the type of kayak and its hull material. The following section explores the different classes of kayaks and provides suggestions on how to maintain these systems.

WHITEWATER KAYAKS

Manufacturers outfit today's whitewater kayaks with a *foam* or *rotomolded pillar system* installed lengthwise into the boat's bow and stern sections. This provides rigidity to the natural flex of a polyethylene hull, allowing it to perform in the water as designed. In the bow, this pillar arrangement prevents the kayak from being crushed by the force of moving water and trapping your feet in the event that the kayak is pinned and submerged. Keep this important safety point in mind before contemplating any modifications to a bow pillar setup.

Designed to be wedged in place and stay there, these pillar systems are relatively maintenance free. Because a seat unit or thigh-brace piece may be helping to hold these pillars in place, check any fasteners holding these parts in for tightness and corrosion. Clean out as best you can any sand, dirt, or debris from around the pillar system. Some kayaks have a bulkhead-type foot brace system. Make sure these are adjusted and firmly in place. Although these pillars provide a certain amount of flotation, installing float bags in any remaining space not used by the paddler and essential gear is a must for serious whitewater paddling. Flotation bag maintenance is discussed in chapter 4.

RECREATIONAL KAYAKS

It's a fundamental rule that all kayaks need adequate flotation. Even a kayak intended for occasional use at the summer-home beach can be easily paddled out into trouble by the wrong person. An empty shell of a kayak filled with water will either sink or float so low in the water it will be virtually useless. Basic entry-level kayaks are the least likely to be adequately equipped as far as bulkheads and flotation are concerned. Manufacturers, responding to a competitive market, economize these add-ons. So it's up to you, the paddler, to assess the kayak's needs for these systems.

At a minimum, both the bow and stern of any kayak should be outfitted with flotation or combination flotation/storage bags. These must be inflated and held in place by foot pegs, the seat back, or the shape of the kayak in such a way that keeps them in place. You don't want them to come floating out at the wrong moment. Combination bags that also hold gear usually lose air faster than float bags and should be checked more frequently. Changing temperatures of hot sun or cool water can greatly affect how snugly these bags stay wedged in place.

Some recreational kayaks come with one bulkhead in the stern, providing a storage area accessible with a hatch. This configuration requires several comments. First, the hatches on such kayaks are often not very watertight; therefore, the storage space may not provide secure flotation. If you're going to paddle any distance, add a backup float or dry bag—even an old inner tube will work. You can check the watertightness of a hatch cover by spraying it with a water hose. Also, polyethylene-hull bulkheads may develop leaks or come loose over time, especially if the boat gets banged around a lot. (Bulkhead repair is discussed in chapter 4.) Equally as important, you still need flotation in the bow. A swamped kayak with flotation in only one end can "buoy" up and be impossible for a paddler in the water to bail out.

Many kayaks in this category have some sort of stiffening rod or support running along the inside of the keel line, usually held in place by the seat unit. Polyethylene hulls with relatively wide, flat bottoms need this support to prevent excessive flexing. Be sure these parts are firmly mounted in place and are not harboring sand, pebbles, and fermented food scraps. A good flotation-bag system can stiffen up the kayak and make it cruise through water more efficiently.

SEA KAYAKS

In the last five years or so, polyethylene sea kayak design and construction has improved dramatically. Better rotomolding techniques allow more precise distribution of the plastic into areas of the hull that need the most stiffness. Slightly narrower, more performance-oriented designs are eliminating flat, excessively flexing keel lines. Leaky bulkheads are not nearly the problem they used to be, but it's still a good idea to check the integrity of bulkheads that have been glued into place. Plastic-welded bulkheads should be nearly maintenance free.

These kayaks are usually equipped with both bow and stern bulkheads for dual flotation and storage. A backup flotation bag in each compartment is recommended if you're paddling empty.

Composite sea kayaks almost always come with factory-installed bulkheads. These are generally trouble free since the composite surface bonds easily with a variety of materials. The water-tightness of the bulkheaded compartments usually depends on the hatch design (see pages 32–33). Lightweight touring kayaks without a bulkhead system will need flotation bags in both ends. Because hand labor is required in laying up a composite hull, there may be occasional rough spots or sharp burrs of resin or exposed cloth, especially if the builder wasn't super meticulous. Hunt for any of these spots and sand or tape them smooth so you don't inadvertently puncture a brand-new set of float bags.

SIT-ON-TOP KAYAKS

The enclosed, one-piece nature of these craft (see illustration on page 18) provides adequate flotation, as long as the hull remains leakproof. Listen for sounds of trapped water when moving the kayak around on land. Fasten-down points for hardware, stiff spots in the hull, such as around drain holes, ribs, or chines, may be points of wear or locations of tiny cracks and sources of leaks. Some sit-on-tops may have threaded access hatches or drain plugs that need to be kept clean. Be equally cautious if renting one of these craft; rental kayaks usually get more abuse than personally owned ones.

FOLDING KAYAKS

The wood or metal frame of folding kayaks provides the rigidity needed for the craft to hold its shape. Preventive maintenance of this framework is a regular part of the ownership of a folding craft. Whenever you assemble or disassemble the frame, make it a habit to scan the pieces for flaws and worn spots. The sooner you repair or protect those pieces the better, so that a weak member doesn't transfer stresses to other sections of the frame. If you leave your kayak in the assembled state for long periods of time, some of the metal joints, *ferrules*, or hinges may seize up. At the very least, periodically flush out the sand and salt residue with fresh water and allow the kayak to completely dry.

The same flotation issues previously discussed are also true for folding kayaks. Some folding designs have built-in interior *sponsons*, or air chambers, along the inside waterline. Additional float bags or dry bags placed in unused spaces are always a good idea.

Deck Accoutrements

The variety of attached kayak accessories range from the standard grab loops to deck lines, stretch cords, hatches, fasteners, and rudder or skeg mechanisms. Whitewater kayaks have a minimum of this paraphernalia, and sea kayaks have the most. Think of your maintenance inspection as an opportunity to check these parts over, as well as make plans for any deck layout modifications or additions.

In general, routine maintenance means checking metal parts for function and corrosion, and checking nylon lines and other synthetic components for wear and UV deterioration. Although a kayak hull may last a decade or even the owner's lifetime, the individual components may need servicing or replacing every couple of years.

GRAB LOOPS OR HANDLES

Virtually all kayaks have grab handles at the ends of the bow and stern. These not only make it easy to move the kayak around the parking lot but also provide a vital handhold during a capsize or rescue operation. They can also do extra duty as tie-down points for cartopping. These handles can be a simple loop of webbing bolted to the deck or a loop of rope passing through a toggle and a sealed hole in the tip of the hull. Usually the nylon wears out first, often from the abrasion of *cartopping* bow and stern lines. Take care when pulling line through the grab loops, as the line can have a cutting or even a melting effect from friction at a stationary point on the loop.

DECK LINES AND BUNGEE CORDS

Sea kayaks usually have several systems of lines attached to the deck in various patterns. An outer perimeter of line, bow and stern, is placed as a grab line for rescue purposes. This consists of nylon or polypropylene cord passing through a series of deck fittings, with recessed fittings being the most durable and trouble free. Other patterns of deck lines, usually done with elastic stretch cord material, are placed to hold down gear such as map cases or spare paddles.

Since these stretch or *bungee* cords are susceptible to UV radiation and exposure to chemicals such as chlorinated water in swimming pools, periodically check them for deterioration. Look for thin spots, especially around the deck fittings, which indicate that the internal strands of elastic are breaking down. If the cords seem to be losing their zip, they are probably approaching retirement age. I have found that these signs of deterioration begin to show up after about two really active paddling seasons. This estimate may be optimistic if you live in the southern latitudes. A regular application of 303 Protectant or similar UV inhibitor on these and other lines should extend their life span.

Nylon cord used for deck lines, painter lines, or towlines is also susceptible to UV degradation, but less so than stretch cords. Polypropylene cord is lighter, suppler, and more UV resistant. When inspecting cords, look for fading, loss of suppleness, and signs of abrasion around deck fittings and other edges. Check plastic deck fittings and cleats for signs of cracking or general wear, and check that the bolts holding them in place are tight and not corroding.

HATCHES

Kayaks with bulkheads require some sort of entry hatch system to gain access to the end compartments, and there are probably as many hatch designs as there are kayak designs. Smaller hatches are usually more waterproof, and larger ones are more convenient to get things in and out of, so how watertight a particular hatch system is involves some compromises.

The only completely waterproof hatch systems are the *VCP-type* round rubber hatches typically used on British-made sea kayaks. These hatches are becoming more common on North American kayaks as well. Their 7.5-inch (19.05 cm) openings, however, are inconvenient to get bulky items, such as camping gear, in and out of. A larger oval cousin to the round hatch seems to be virtually as secure and partially solves the access problem. Both oval and round rubber hatches are generally pretty free of problems, although the covers' rubber compound can deteriorate with exposure to UV radiation and atmospheric pollutants. Extend their life with a periodic coating with a UV inhibitor. Also, keep sand out of the inner grooves and away from the lip of the hatch opening.

North American–made kayaks use larger rectangular and trapezoidal-shaped hatches, which are easier to get gear in and out of, but will usually let small amounts of water seep in when paddling in rough conditions. Hatch systems are improving; it's the older designs that tend to leak the worst. The newest designs have *camming buckles* and straps on the outside that put downward pressure on the hatch cover. These hatches work fairly well if adequate tension is kept on the straps and you give the gasket or seal some routine care. Keep sand and dirt out, store the kayak with the hatch unfastened to reduce compression of the gasket, and give the cover a periodic coating with a UV inhibitor.

Hatches on polyethylene kayaks commonly include a neoprene cover that fits over the hatch opening like a neoprene spray skirt on the coaming. A polyethylene hard cover then fits over that to hold the neoprene down securely. This system will work reasonably well if you keep the neoprene cover's draw cord properly tensioned. Protect it from the sun as much as possible and remove it from the hatch opening when storing the kayak.

RUDDERS AND SKEGS

Rudders and skegs are popular features on many sea kayak models and on some shorter recreational kayaks as well. They are also the mechanism on kayaks most prone to problems. Rudders (moveable blades, dropped from the boat's stern) with their exposed parts are liable to be tangled or damaged in a number of ways, and the blades can be bent or broken if deployed in shallow areas upon landing. Skegs (fixed blades that generally drop from a slot inside the hull) are also vulnerable during landing and can occasionally get jammed with pebbles picked up while being dragged on a beach. We will discuss these issues in more detail in chapter 4.

As far as basic maintenance goes, first check the control cables for smooth and easy movement and look for any signs of fraying where the cable exits the hull or makes a bend. A shot of a silicone lubricant into cable channels may improve the ease of movement as well as repel water. Check for excess play in the blades or rudder housings and, if possible, eliminate this sloppiness by tightening things up or by installing plastic bushings or corrosion-proof washers to take up any slack. Wobbling blades cause the kayak to wander off course, dissipate forward motion, and

A skeg retracts in and out of a slot in the stern section of the hull. This slot needs to be kept free of sand and pebbles.

A typical sea kayak rudder setup with the blade in the retracted position. The cable to the foot controls can wear and fray at the point where it enters the hull.

invite *pumping* the foot controls, creating further drag.

Check other moving parts for ease of motion and be certain that any bolts, screws, or springs are adequately tight but can be loosened in case a field repair is necessary. Look over the condition of the rudder or skeg blade and file or sand smooth any burrs or dings that might catch seaweed or other debris, causing drag. If any replacement parts are needed, plan ahead because they may need to be special-ordered from the manufacturer.

Maintaining Accessories

The paddle (and a spare) is your means of propulsion and is the next most important piece of gear. Your spray skirt or *spray deck* is a vital link between you and your boat, creating the sealed system necessary for serious kayaking. Most of the rest of the gear we will discuss is part of your safety system. PFDs, flotation bags, throw ropes, pumps, and so on minimize the seriousness of any mishaps and allow you to help yourself and your paddling partners get out of trouble. Keeping all these pieces of gear in good working condition cannot be overemphasized.

Paddles

Your paddle will see more active use and undergo more stresses, bumps, and bangs than any of the rest of your gear. The tip and edges of the blades receive the most abuse, a good portion of which comes at launching when using the paddle to push off from shore. Look for worn spots, chips, and small cracks. These can usually be sanded smooth and touched up with epoxy in the case of composite-blade pad-

Typical wear and tear of a fiberglass paddle blade.

Tip damage of carbon-fiber-laminate paddle caused primarily by beach launching.

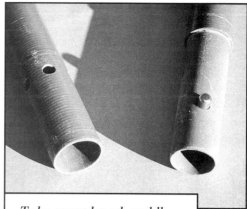

Take-apart kayak paddle ferrules should be cleaned of sand and salt.

dles, and with varnish or oil in the case of wood paddles. We discuss this further on page 63 in chapter 4, the "repair chapter." Repair *delaminations* or cracks that look like they are going to travel further along the grain or material before using the paddle again.

Are the blades still mounted securely into the shaft? A loose blade will have to be repositioned and reglued. Look closely for any stress cracks at points where the blades will flex, such as at the end of a stiffening rib extending from the shaft. Feel along the shaft of the paddle for nicks or gouges that may irritate your hands while paddling, and touch them up with a fine grit sandpaper.

Take-apart joints on most paddles require some periodic maintenance. First, clean any sand or debris from the surfaces of the joint and the exposed insides of the shaft. Check the *control button* for proper operation. When the two halves are assembled, twist each side a bit to feel for looseness or sloppiness. With regular use, most take-apart joints develop some play; this can easily be remedied (see page 64).

Occasionally, water gets into hollow paddle shafts. You will be able to hear it trickling back and forth as you rotate the paddle. Try to find the leak where the water is getting in, and if possible, position the paddle so that the water will percolate back out. Then seal up the leak. In a more stubborn case, refer to pages 64–65.

Paddle scratches on the sides of the kayak ahead of the cockpit are another issue. If you find yourself hitting the sides of the kayak with any regularity, it may be time to reassess your paddling style. You may need to get more of your upper body involved with reaching and placing the paddle properly in the water for the forward stroke. The length of your paddle and the width of your boat may be factors, as well. Seek some advice from a paddling instructor or knowledgeable paddlesports shop.

Certain types of paddle damage, such as delaminations or clean breaks, may be warranty issues. Check with the shop where you got the paddle or contact the manufacturer. Warranty coverage is certainly a gray area, as no paddle is indestructible in all paddling conditions. A number of the better quality paddle makers offer various repair or replacement options at an additional price. Though a bit expensive, this form of product insurance is less costly than a new paddle. If you find yourself regularly paddling in one of the extreme zones of kayaking, such as rock-studded creeks or heavy surf, and your paddle is overflexing, groaning, or otherwise getting beat up, it's probably time to get a bombproof, specialized paddle for that purpose and retain your old, general-purpose cruiser for the easy miles.

PFDs

Like your kayak and paddle, it's essential that your PFD be seaworthy every time you go out on the water. Your first thought may be "What can go wrong with a PFD?" The answer is: a lot. The following are some things to look at to get the longest amount of service out of this piece of equipment.

First, check the various functioning components—the zipper or zippers and waist belt or other fit-adjusting straps. Is everything in smooth working order and free of sand? Then inspect the fabric panels, looking for spots of mildew or excessive ground-in dirt. Fading on the exposed back and shoulders indicates UV degradation of the nylon. Poke at the fabric in those areas to see if it's retaining its resiliency or is beginning to fray and split. Fabric damage can also occur at the lower edges of a PFD where it may rub and abrade on the spray skirt. When the PFD is being transported or stored for any length of time, avoid cinching it down with a strap or putting heavy objects on top of it. Compressing the foam decreases its buoyancy.

When any of the internal foam flotation pieces are poking through, as if about to make their escape, it's obviously time to retire the vest. Small spots of damage may be glueable or patchable, but fabric deterioration from UV is pretty much terminal. Basic preventive maintenance includes periodic washings in fresh water with nondetergent soap and drying. Hanging the PFD up to dry completely after each trip and improvising drying methods when out of the water during the long ones are important. Also, there are a number of good fabric-washing and rejuvenating products on the market (see page 67).

The value of a PFD as a safety device is only as good as the fit. It only works if it stays on when you're in the water. If it no longer fits—maybe you got a new kayak with a different-fitting spray skirt, you have donned a bulky new garment like a drysuit, or you just ate too many pizzas over the winter season—then it's time to get a new PFD.

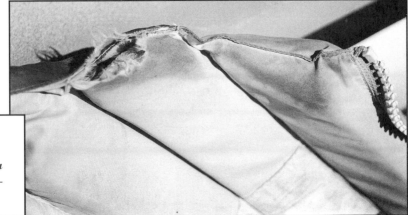

UV and mildew damage to the nylon fabric on a PFD. Time to retire this one.

Spray Skirts

As with the PFD, periodically check your spray skirt closely for fabric degradation. Most of the wear and tear occurs on the surfaces that are in contact with the cockpit coaming, especially on fiberglass coamings that may have sharper edges. Touch up spots of abrasion in these areas with a flexible sealant like AquaSeal. Nylon and neoprene skirts may show signs of UV deterioration, especially in the forward deck area of the skirt where the fabric is most exposed and under the most tension. Most

Deterioration of neoprene and nylon spray skirts from age and UV exposure usually first occurs where the fabric is stretched over the coaming.

models of skirts have an elastic cord built into the perimeter, to allow for adjusting the tightness of the fit on the coaming. Every now and then check this fit and verify that the knot or fastener that holds this tension is secure.

Spray skirts can develop leaks at the fabric's seams. Neoprene seams are either glued or stitched and glued and are usually watertight unless the rubber is tearing away from the seam. Nylon skirts are sewn, and the better quality ones are then *seam taped*. Make sure that this tape is not peeling away, creating a leak point. Seams that have been sealed by hand with a seam glue will need periodic touch-ups every year or so. To test these seams, try pooling some water on the fabric over the seam for a few minutes. A well-sealed seam won't allow water to drip through.

While looking the skirt over, see if it has an adequate grab loop for pulling the skirt loose during wet exits and fast exits of surf landings. You may want to tie in an extra loop, a large knot, or a plastic ball that will provide a quick, easy grip with cold hands or without looking.

Accelerated deterioration can happen to spray skirts, especially neoprene, that have seen practice duty in a chlorinated swimming pool. It may be most economical to buy a cheap skirt for practice in pools.

Clothing

As with your other fabric-based gear, the most important thing you can do with your paddling clothing is to keep it dry between uses. Soggy jackets or wetsuits left fermenting in the bilge of your kayak or in the trunk of your car are the perfect recipe for an unpleasant start to the next trip. Mildews and other microorganisms that like damp, dark places can deteriorate many fabrics and their waterproof coatings. At the very least, the rank odors of perpetually damp gear can be next to impossible to wash away.

So the first thing to do after and even during a trip is to get your wet duds hanging up and dried out. Regular in-season washings are the next step toward prolonging the life of these garments. Manufacturer's care instructions are a good starting point when planning your periodic washing routine, which may mean keeping for reference the hangtags you got when items were new. In general, you can safely hand wash most items in warm or cool water using a nondetergent, low-sudsing cleaner, such as Woolite or a specialized outdoor gear–cleaning agent. Be sure to do a thorough rinse job and dry thoroughly. Good water-repellency-renewing products are discussed on pages 67–70.

Once your paddle clothing is clean and approachable without a clothespin on your nose, you can look for other signs of wear. Abrasion holes or tears from mishaps on the river or on the beach need to be fixed as soon as possible. Quick fixes can be done with fabric repair tape or even duct tape, but these are only temporary measures. You can make permanent repairs to nylon fabrics by sewing and seam sealing. As with spray skirts, seams in coated nylon fabrics are factory seam taped or require manual seam sealing. Follow the directions on these sealants and allow plenty of time for them to cure properly. Small tears or holes in neoprene items can be fixed relatively easily, usually without sewing. Specialized fabrics such as Gore-Tex will probably require getting the item to a Gore-authorized repair center. Chapter 4 discusses renewing the durable waterproof layer, a treatment done to most waterproof/breathable fabrics.

The *latex seals* on paddle jackets and drysuits need special attention. Although providing the security of totally waterproof seals, latex is a relatively fragile, fickle material, susceptible to sharp finger- and toenails, body sweat, chlorine, UV radiation, suntan lotions, insect repellents, ozone, and even rough beard hairs. Such outside conditions can work in collusion to blow these seals out. Inspect these seals regularly and meticulously to find any small nicks, tears, or signs of cracking that may cause you trouble when you least need it. Manufacturers using latex seals recommend monthly applications of a preservative such as 303 Protectant. In the not-too-distant future, there will probably be some more durable alternative, but for now, keeping dry on the water means a lot of monkey business at other times to maintain the seals.

Latex seals and booties need to be treated periodically with an oxidation and UV inhibitor.

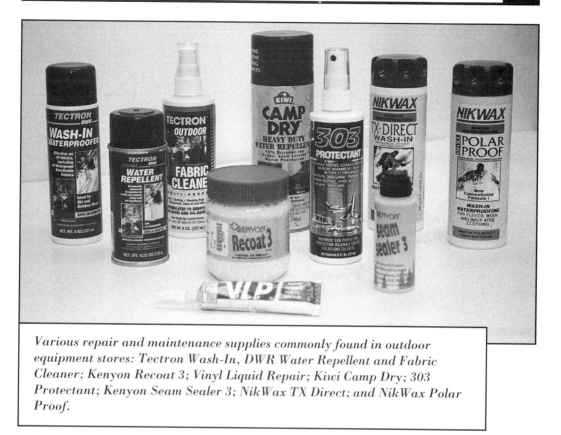

Various repair and maintenance supplies commonly found in outdoor equipment stores: Tectron Wash-In, DWR Water Repellent and Fabric Cleaner; Kenyon Recoat 3; Vinyl Liquid Repair; Kiwi Camp Dry; 303 Protectant; Kenyon Seam Sealer 3; NikWax TX Direct; and NikWax Polar Proof.

New latex seals may be quite tight and difficult to put on, and a tight fit around the neck may be particularly uncomfortable at first. Manufacturers may or may not recommend that the seals be trimmed to fit, but do so judiciously and with caution. If you trim too much, you will diminish the effectiveness of the seal, and any nicks or irregularities in the cut can lead to splits later. It's best to give the latex a chance to stretch naturally with use or to stretch it over an appropriate round object for a period of time.

Baby drysuit zippers and avoid folding and compressing the suit as much as possible when it's not in use or while being transported. Store the zipper in a fully closed position. Special zipper lubricants, such as Zip Care from McNett, help keep the zippers sliding freely. Be cautious about using paraffin or other waxes; they may be too efficient and allow the zipper to pop open unexpectedly.

FOOTWEAR

The popular sports sandals are ubiquitous in the outdoor world, and, unless you have very little room for bulky footwear in the bow of your boat, they work well for many kayaking applications in the summer or when the water is warm. Maybe it's just easier to trip on things when wearing them, but I seem to get more delaminations with sandals than other types of footwear. But these are easy to fix with a flexible adhesive such as Freesole or Barge Cement. You can use a soap called Sandal Suds if you really like to keep them clean.

Neoprene boots or socks provide more insulation but are some of the hardest articles to keep clean and dry. The best thing you can do is to give them plenty of ventilation between uses to keep them as dry as possible. Keep a bent coat hanger or broomstick handy to prop them open. While doing this, check the soles, toes, heels, and insoles for wear or delaminations, and note them for possible repair. An enzyme-based cleaner, Sink the Stink, seems to do a good job dissolving odors in neoprene and other synthetic fabrics.

Emergency and Rescue Equipment

Both whitewater and sea kayaking have an assortment of rescue accessories that need to be kept in top condition. Throw ropes and towline systems require a working component of rope that should be kept clean and inspected for possible damage after each serious use. These systems are usually made up of either polypropylene or *Spectra rope* or perhaps a blend of the two. Extremely strong and light, Spectra appears in the high-end "pro" rescue bags. Polypropylene is also light and usually suffices for boat-to-boat towing and other general duty use. Though strong, nylon rope is heavy and not buoyant, which limits its use to land-based operations.

These ropes can come in either a *braided* or *kernmantle* construction. Braided rope is easy to inspect for cuts and abrasion, as all the strands are visible. Kernmantle construction utilizes an outer sheath protecting an inner load-bearing core. These ropes are very durable and have a nice feel to them, but it's possible for the core to be damaged and not visible from the outside. Ropes used in a serious rescue effort may have approached their load capacities and should probably be retired or "repurposed" to less demanding uses.

Like other types of fabric or nylon-based gear, throw ropes and towlines can be washed in warm water with a nondetergent soap, and then spread out to dry. The bags, packs, or pouches used to store them should be checked for tearing seams, loose knots, or balky closures. Rescue hardware, such as *carabiners* and pulleys, should operate smoothly and be free of corrosion. Make sure the carabiners and their kid brothers, the *mini-biners*, that you have set aside for rescue operations are specifically designed for paddlesports purposes.

Helmets are essential for whitewater paddling as well as serious surf paddling—in other words, any time you're deliberately playing around in quickly moving water with shallow conditions. The key to effective helmet performance is proper fit. Most helmets have a padding system that controls the way it fits your head. Make sure the helmet remains securely in place and, if you're going to wear a cap or neoprene hood underneath, that it's readjusted and ready to go. Closely inspect and be prepared to retire any helmet that has undergone an impact. Check the manufacturer's recommendations or replacement policies.

Sea kayaking has a number of safety and signaling accessories used for coastal and open-water paddling situations. Coast Guard requirements necessitate carrying an approved set of signaling devices as well as a bright light for night travel. The three-packs of handheld or hand-fired signal flares commonly carried by kayakers satisfy this requirement. Being explosive devices, proper care and use of them is essential. Read all directions and warnings and be familiar with their use. The catch is that it's illegal and ill-advised to fire these things in nonemergency situations, so practice is impossible. Occasionally, the various sea kayak symposiums will have clinics on this topic, and perhaps a Coast Guard facility in your area could arrange for a group or club practice session. Monitor the stated expiration dates of these flare products and keep them as dry as possible and stored away from extreme heat and cold. Other specialized safety and special-use accessories are discussed in chapter 5.

A flashlight is an essential piece of equipment for any paddle tour in which there is a chance of being out at night. Any light with a bright, white beam will satisfy the coastal requirement for paddlecraft. A number of good waterproof, handheld or *headlamp-style lights* are available from camping suppliers or paddlesports and dive shops. Check the local regulations in your area before investing in a blinking strobe light. In some waters, a flashing light is considered a distress signal. Waterproof lights are mostly maintenance-free, but you should remove batteries when not on a trip to prevent corrosion from leaking battery acid. Occasionally check the condition of the *O-ring seals*, and touch them up with a tiny bit of silicone grease if they get stiff.

Don't forget about your first-aid kit. It's easy to haul one around year after year and not pay any attention to it until it's needed. Remember to replace immediately any items used, and at least once a year evaluate each component to check its condition. Even more important is to know what all that stuff is for. Many clubs, outdoor stores, paddlesports shops, and kayak symposiums have occasional first aid and wilderness care–related clinics, a very good investment in time before you venture onto the water.

Compasses and Electronics

For serious sea kayakers, a deck compass is a standard piece of navigational equipment. But do you know how accurate it is? We will discuss ways to check the compass against a known bearing for reference in chapter 4. Some marine compasses have magnetic adjustments for correcting error. This is a tricky process, so follow directions carefully if you have one of those. A small discrepancy of a few degrees can be tolerated for most paddlers' needs over relatively short distances. A *sighting compass* or *GPS* (global positioning system) can be used for precise navigational work.

VHF radios and GPS navigational instruments are becoming increasingly popular for all types of serious paddling. As with all electronics, the technology is changing rapidly, and prices are coming down. Continual care of these devices while on the water is necessary if you want to get the most use from them. Read through directions, obviously, and be aware of any warranty limitations. To use such equipment effectively requires skills that take practice.

From the maintenance standpoint, be cautious of any claims of waterproofness in relation to electronic gadgets. Find out exactly how the manufacturer is defining *waterproof, water-resistant,* or *submersible*. I have heard enough stories about soggy, dead instruments that were supposedly waterproof. So take as many precautions as possible. Several good waterproof accessory bags are on the market that will provide security. Battery compartments are often the weak link as far as waterproofness is concerned. Check these seals periodically and keep them clean. After any exposure to salt water, rinse with freshwater and dry thoroughly.

Dry Bags, Flotation Bags, and Waterproof Containers

There are as many brands and styles of dry bags and flotation bags available as there are kayaks and paddles. All sorts of sizes, shapes, and materials can fulfill most flotation or waterproof storage needs, from carrying your keys to protecting a month's worth of provisions. Maintenance of these bags boils down to a few general principles. Vinyl or PVC bags are generally the least expensive and the heaviest. Urethane-coated nylon bags are lighter, more abrasion resistant, and more expensive. Vynabond, Aquaseal, or similar urethane adhesives can touch up or patch these materials.

Over time, all dry bags develop worn spots at edges, corners, and wrinkles. These can eventually wear through, becoming small pinhole leaks. Seams of bags with stitched and/or glued seams can also develop leaks. Electronically welded seams in the newer generation of dry bags tend to be largely free of leakage. One way to test for watertightness is to seal the bag and give it a steady hug or squeeze, while listening for escaping air. If the bag is airtight, it should be watertight for a reasonable length of time. To be even more meticulous, you can hold the sealed bag under water in a sink or bathtub and look for a telltale string of bubbles to identify a leak point. Mark the spot for repair when the bag is dry. Give larger areas of abrasion a preventive coating of urethane adhesive.

There are several types of closures on dry bags, the most popular being the roll-up-and-buckle type of closure. Don't overstuff these bags, or it will be impossible to roll down the top with enough turns to get a tight seal. Squeezing the bag will tell you if air is escaping or if you have a good seal. Drawing a "fill line" on the bag makes it easier for you to see when to stop putting things in.

Some dry bags, such as those from Voyageur, have a long slide-on clip that provides a very secure seal but is harder to stow in small spaces. They work best in kayaks that have only one or no bulkheads and where flotation is also needed. Also, some storage bags utilize a special waterproof zipper similar to the ones used in drysuits. These are relatively easy to get stuff out of, such as cameras when you're in a hurry, but the zipper makes them fairly expensive.

All of these closure systems should be kept clean and free of sand for best operation. Occasionally, completely empty the bags and allow them to dry and air out. If you plan to use a set of dry bags for overnight camping in critter country—and there are critters just about everywhere—be sure to wash thoroughly bags used for food storage to minimize food odors. I usually rotate my oldest, nearly worn-out bags into food or garbage duty, so if some little—or not so little—forest friend chews its way in, I won't have to mourn the loss of a brand-new bag.

Most types of flotation bags and some flotation/storage bags come with built-in air hose systems or pressure release valves that help to keep the bags properly inflated and wedged in place. On long trips, you can squeeze air out to save space. In some extremes of temperature, you may need to release pressure to avoid stressing the bags. When outfitting a kayak with float bags, make sure the air hoses are long enough so you can reach them conveniently for those adjustments. Remember that when adding air by mouth into a storage bag, you're adding a lot of humidity, which may cause condensation inside the bag. Those hoses and valves can also take a beating on the floor of the kayak, so try to keep them tucked out of the way and free of sand and dirt.

A variety of rigid containers with suitable watertight covers or lids can be added to the arsenal of dry storage alternatives. Whether canister- or box-shaped, these are great for items you don't want completely squashed, and they may come with internal padding for gear like cameras or binoculars. Many of these containers, such as the Pelican line, are made of virtually indestructible plastic. The gasket inside the lid provides the watertight seal. Keep this gasket clean and follow the manufacturer's suggestions for touch-up maintenance. Give your empty, dry boxes a submersion test on occasion to check for leakage.

Setting Up a Maintenance Area for Gear

As previously discussed, the hardest part about properly maintaining your paddling gear is developing the habit of doing it on a regular basis. Having adequate work and storage area for your gear makes this chore a lot simpler and helps avoid the temptation of leaving your dirty, wet gear in a heap in your trunk or on the floor of the garage. A designated section of a garage is probably the ideal spot, with a kayak accessories storage rack at working level.

Many paddlers won't have the luxury of that amount of space, so a corner of a reasonably dry basement, a laundry room, a porch, or even a closet can be made to do. The key thing is to be able to sort through gear quickly and hang things up to dry.

Have a small clothesline or some hooks and plastic coat hangers set up to hang wet items on. Keep some basic supplies handy on a shelf where you can easily get them as you unpack from a trip, and be ready to do a few quick fixes before the problems are forgotten. Screwdrivers, pliers, a brush, some rags, and the inevitable roll of duct tape are some of these items. A small plug-in hand vacuum or an old spare vacuum cleaner with an extension hose is great for getting sand out of all kinds of corners after things are dry. Try propping up some broom handles or other long pegs to hang empty dry bags and footwear to dry.

Keep your spray bottle of UV inhibitor available for giving an occasional coating to those latex seals, map cases, decks, and other paraphernalia. (A meticulously organized person—the same kind of person who keeps track of automobile mileage, tire changes, and oil changes in a little notebook kept in the glove box—might keep a list in the workshop or attached to the kayak workstand of the dates of when these items were done, but that's probably too much to ask of most of us.) You may also want to keep a file of the care instructions (along with warranties) of important pieces of equipment. That way, a quick reference will be possible before you use the wrong kind of cleaning material or put off doing anything for lack of knowing what to do. Also hold onto any fabric swatches that come with your paddle garments. Place items in need of more serious repairs in a separate location for later attention. Putting them aside and temporarily out of commission prevents hauling them back out on another trip until they are fixed.

Once you have done these basics, you have doubly earned that cold one, and you can relax in a guilt-free state of satisfaction.

Winter and Summer Storage of Gear

In most parts of the country, kayaking is a seasonal sport. Winter ice on lakes and rivers shuts it down in the northern states and provinces. Whitewater kayaking is subject to seasonal rains and/or releases of water on dam-controlled flowages. Extreme heat and/or humidity in the southernmost states can make paddling an intermittent activity in the summer months. So chances are that you will need to store your kayak and other gear for extended periods of time.

The three major things to take into account when storing any gear are moisture, heat, and extreme cold. Putting things away dry is the most important step, and cleaning them first helps achieve this. Extremes of temperature may or may not have adverse effects on many pieces of gear, but expansion and contraction processes can put stresses on anything made with a combination of dissimilar materials.

First, let's look at storing kayaks. After you have cleaned out the sand, old energy bar wrappers and wet T-shirts, open up any hatches and deflate float bags to allow air circulation. Getting all moisture out is especially important if the kayak will be stored in subfreezing temperatures, to prevent cracking and breakage from freezing and thawing of water. Now is a good time to coat any hatch seals, deck lines, or similar parts with a UV inhibitor to minimize deterioration from automotive exhaust or other atmospheric chemicals. Suspend or cradle the kayak rather than leave it on the ground or on a concrete floor, where it could pick up dampness and scratches from dirt. Hanging it from a set of slings or setting it in a shaped cradle is an ideal solution. If the kayak must be stored outside, cover it with a tarp or shield it somehow from sunlight, but allow for air circulation underneath to prevent condensation.

Composite hulls are naturally stiff and in most cases can be safely suspended from their grab loops, although the sling/cradle idea prevents any possible stresses on the loops. Polyethylene-hull kayaks will require a little bit more TLC. As an elastic, naturally flexible material, polyethylene can deform gradually over time into a shape you don't want. Do not hang your poly kayak by the grab loops; use the sling or cradle system, suspending the boat at about the one-third points or at the bulkheads. Suspending polyethylene kayaks on their side provides more structural rigidity. And avoid extremely hot conditions. Many freestanding garages or sheds can reach critically hot temperatures in the summer months. At the very least, hang the kayak down low in the garage to avoid the most extreme heat.

Folding kayaks are probably best stored disassembled. The unassembly process allows you to look for any parts needing attention and to clean and dry them thoroughly. Wooden hull kayaks should be cleaned, scratches or gashes attended to, and kept away from fluctuations in temperature, humidity, and hibernating rodents.

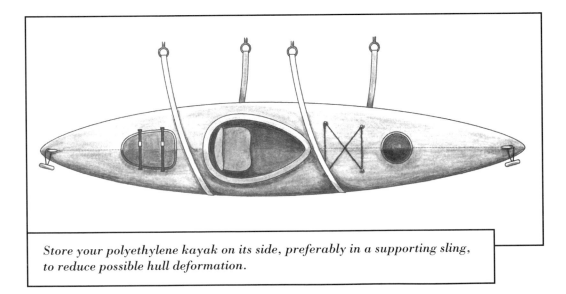

Store your polyethylene kayak on its side, preferably in a supporting sling, to reduce possible hull deformation.

Accessory Storage Tips

- Wood paddles in particular should not be stored in excessively hot locations since they could over time dry out and become more brittle. When first using a wood paddle that has been in storage for awhile and may have gotten dried out, go easy on it for a few days while it regains some humidity and becomes more flexible.

- Paddles with take-apart joints, especially metal ones, should be disassembled so the joint doesn't stick or seize up.

- Combat mildew—the major enemy of anything made with fabrics—by keeping your sewn gear dry and ventilated.

- Deflate air bags to eliminate expansion/contraction cycles. I like to try to remove extra moisture by warming them in the sun and then deflating. Although this latter technique is probably not a real priority, it cuts down on mildew.

- In the frigid cold of a northern winter, when temperatures drop below 0°F (–20°C), materials such as vinyl and neoprene can get stiff and even brittle if kept in unheated storage. Be sure these items will remain undisturbed, or bring them in the house.

- Flashlights, headlamps, radios, and any similar instrument should have the batteries removed, and be thoroughly cleaned of any salt residue. Store these items in the house, rather than the garage or vehicle, to minimize the corrosive effects of moisture.

- Don't forget that if little nuisance critters, mainly rodents, can get at your gear, they can wreak havoc. I once saw a polyethylene touring kayak after a squirrel decided it needed an emergency exit: the result was an ugly, unrepairable hole in the stern. Mice and squirrels will gnaw on wood paddles to get at the salt flavor and will chew their way into anything with food odors.

4

REPAIRING BOATS AND EQUIPMENT

In chapter 3, we looked at the basic maintenance needs of kayaks and other gear. Even with the most loving care, the most precise technique, and the most careful planning, our paddling possessions are going to get scratched, dog-eared, dented, cracked, punctured, torn, abraded, corroded, and eventually, pretty worn out. When this inevitable wear and tear is likely to affect the performance of the piece of gear, or the condition is likely to get worse, then it is time to do some repairs.

Minor repairs done routinely will prevent major repairs later and perhaps prevent an untimely end to a trip or even an accident. Periodic attention to detail also means getting the greatest value out of the life of the product and avoiding the unnecessary expense of replacing another throwaway. You can take a certain pride in keeping major pieces of gear—which are sort of old friends—serviceable as long as possible.

Most of the repair work discussed in this chapter is doable for the average person. Perhaps the hardest part of the process, like keeping up a regular exercise schedule, is making up your mind to do it. However, once you are committed to prolonging the life of your kayak and accessories, gathering up the correct tools and supplies and organizing your workspace can be part of a satisfying process. I find it most efficient to do a number of repair projects in one work session. If you have the luxury of a permanent workspace or workshop, that's great! If not, then the time spent carefully organizing the work area will pay off in a better repair job.

Working outdoors on a nice day can be an ideal work space. You will have adequate light and plenty of ventilation if using adhesives or solvents. Be sure to allow enough time for cleanup and for any changes in the weather. Garages and carports can provide some shelter and still have plenty of fresh air. Indoor space should be well lit and ventilated. Wherever you work, position your boat or other gear at a comfortable height so you don't have to kneel or bend at the waist.

Have all your tools and materials assembled and ready. If you are working with a kit or using adhesives or chemicals, read through the directions to familiarize yourself about any cautions and emergency procedures. Have your glasses or protective eyewear handy, and consider wearing rubber or latex gloves as well. Make certain that children or pets are supervised or out of harm's way, especially while chemicals are present or adhesives are curing.

If you are uncomfortable about doing any of these projects yourself or cutting off a strip of duct tape in a straight line is challenging for you, there are other ways to accomplish these chores. Some of the better paddlesports specialty retailers offer repair services or know of local contacts who can do the work. Marina shops that work on fiberglass may be willing to take on a kayak. Shipping expenses normally prohibit returning a kayak to the original manufacturer, but this may be an option in cases of extensive damage or to maintain the warranty. This option is likely time-consuming and is best considered in the off-season.

Manufacturers of paddlesports accessories often offer repair services for their products, usually for a reasonable charge. Damage to products from normal use is not likely to be covered by warranties, but if you have an unusual break or crack, any kind of delamination, or a seam coming apart, it is worthwhile to check into what the warranty covers. Having the sales receipt available makes this process easier for all concerned.

Local paddling clubs or outfitters are another source for repair advice and help. Most active clubs have a few knowledgeable gurus who will happily give advice or maybe even help with a project. Perhaps if you offer to help organize a club maintenance and repair day or event, you can get like-minded paddlers together, get some work done, and have a great time. Likewise, outfitters and *liveries*, who are regularly doing maintenance to their own fleets, may be willing to contribute advice or assistance.

Hull Repairs

There is a pecking order of sorts as to prioritizing repairs. Fixing a leaky or damaged kayak is going to be high on the to-do list. The first step is to decide what it is that needs to be done. Minor surface scratches and abrasion are generally a cosmetic issue, and how close to "new" you want your boat to look will determine what, if anything, needs to be done. Any cracked, gouged, or torn spot that leaks or probably will leak if impacted again should be repaired as soon as possible. And any catastrophic damage that has compromised the kayak's shape, rigidity, or seaworthiness must be evaluated and fixed immediately. If your kayak seems to look or paddle differently than it did previously, and you are not sure what's wrong, seek a professional opinion before using it again. Also, because of the variety of materials used in kayak construction, several potential repair procedures may be necessary. The next sections look at these various alternatives for each of the kayak hull materials.

Polyethylene Hulls

As the toughest hull material used to make kayaks, a polyethylene hull is the least likely to sustain damage that puts the boat out of service. A well-used polyethylene kayak, one that has had lots of contact with river, beach, or shoreline rocks, will sport an extensive pattern of scrapes and gouges, eventually giving the bottom a fuzzy feel. This surface wear is inevitable and won't affect the integrity of the hull. It is debatable how much this rough surface will slow down the hull as it glides through the water but shouldn't be a big concern since these kayaks are made primarily for recreational use.

Some of the more pronounced of these *polyethylene "fuzzies"* can be reduced by trimming carefully with a sharp knife or by going over the surface carefully with a sharp, steel ski-base scraper. Some manufacturers suggest using sandpaper, in progressively finer grades, but the original smooth surface will prove elusive to duplicate. If you try any of these methods, proceed slowly and avoid taking off any more material than you have to.

Of greater concern are concentrated spots of wear that may develop under a stiff interior structure such as a seat or bulkhead. A thin spot or hole can possibly result if the wear and tear can't be avoided. It may be possible to shift the positions of these interior parts, especially if they are removable. It may also be possible to wedge a stiffening material such as minicell foam or an aluminum or Plexiglas sheet between the interior part and the inside of the hull to spread out the load at this pressure point.

Deeper gouges or punctures are unlikely unless you hit something quite sharp, typically of human origin. Holes and leaks in polyethylene hulls are difficult to repair, but not impossible; the dilemma is finding something that will adhere to the synthetic surface. Many poly kayaks with such leaks finish out their serviceable years patched up with successive applications of duct tape. This works temporarily since duct tape only lasts a season at the most. Be sure to patch the inside as well as the outside of the hull. The tape will adhere better if you first clean the area around the leak with solvent alcohol. Another down-and-dirty plug for a small hole is to install a stainless steel nut and bolt with washers large enough to cover the damaged area and placed on both sides of the hull. To prevent corrosion, do not mix different types of metal. Also, this bolt method is impractical in the high wear area on the bottom of the hull.

A more permanent patching option that may work on cuts and small holes is the use of a two-part urethane adhesive or a polyurethane caulk, such as Lexel, available at most complete hardware stores. Thoroughly clean the surface to be worked on and follow the directions and cautions that come with each product. Lexel caulk is paintable if you want to try to get a color match. Use a putty knife or other smooth edge lubricated with soapy water to form a smooth surface.

The only really secure patch on a polyethylene hull involves the use of plastic welding techniques. These methods include cleaning and preheating the hull and then heat-bonding the plastic filler or patch into place. A heat gun or propane torch is needed, and the correct range of temperatures is relatively important for the plastic to bond but not burn. Polyethylene in a P-Tex ski-base repair stick may be adequate for simple patching projects. I have heard varying amounts of success with this technique as a do-it-yourself project.

A more professional job can be done with plastic-welding machinery, which can be effective on both *linear* and *cross-linked* polyethylene *surfaces*. Such equipment is beyond the budget of most paddlers, but many outfitters and other repair centers can do these repairs. To follow up on this alternative, check with the manufacturer of your kayak or contact Jack's Plastic Welding, listed in chapter 8, for more leads.

Warps, sometimes referred to as *wows*, are the polyethylene-hull problem most likely to affect paddling efficiency. Polyethylene is a fairly elastic material, and its shape can be distorted by exposure to heat or pressure. These problems mostly occur when the kayak is on land and the hull is not supported with its weight distributed evenly, such as when left on a storage rack in the sun or tied tightly to a vehicle rack. These distortions can cause the boat to increase in *rocker* (the built-in curvature in a boat's hull from bow to stern—see text and illustration on page 4),

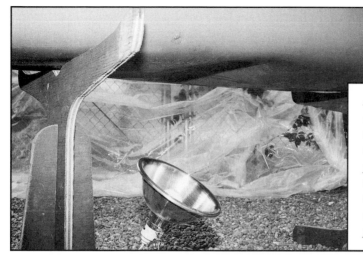

A patient, controlled dose of heat and pressure can often reduce or eliminate deformities in polyethylene hulls. A weight such as a brick can be used on the inside of the hull to help the process.

making it track poorly, and if warped to one side, make it difficult to turn in one direction. Successive waves of ripples in the bottom of the hull can cause uneven wear patterns and decrease the efficiency of the hull while gliding through the water.

Fortunately, molded polyethylene has a *memory* or the ability to return to its original shape when opposite forces are applied. If you have a kayak with some such distortion in its shape, controlled exposure to pressure and heat can correct the problem. First, try to identify the problem and determine what forces caused it. A wow in the deck or hull will be obvious and sometimes just leaving the kayak in the warm sun or in a warm garage allows the dent to ease back into shape. If this doesn't work, try some steady pressure on the convex side of the problem area. Do this by positioning the kayak in some way that allows you to place a weight, such as a brick, on the area. When positioning your kayak in this fashion, don't compound your problems by creating another pressure point elsewhere. Keep the kayak warm and check on it regularly. A heat source, such as a lightbulb or hair dryer, can speed up the process, but don't exceed a too-hot-to-touch temperature.

A series of wows in the hull may be caused by a decrease in the amount of rocker, and conversely, an increase in rocker can result from lengthy hanging from the grab loops. Determining how much rocker your kayak was intended to have may be difficult unless you can compare yours to a new one, perhaps at your dealer. With the kayak on a flat surface you can measure the rise in the keel line at some points near the bow and stern. Hang your distorted kayak in some fashion to reverse the bend and hope for the best. Be patient; these warping problems occur gradually, and correcting them will take some time as well.

You can determine a side-to-side distortion by tying a straight base line with string lengthwise above the kayak and carefully comparing it to the long axis of the boat. Hanging the kayak on the appropriate side in a center sling or support with weights on the end may reduce this distortion. I have seen brand-new kayaks delivered right from the manufacturer with these problems, so carefully look over any polyethylene kayak you buy to avoid these troubles to begin with. Then, to avoid trouble in the future, heed some of the cartopping and storage considerations discussed elsewhere.

Catastrophic damage that renders a polyethylene hull unusable is rare. Probably the worst-case scenario is the swamped kayak that gets wrapped around a rock or bridge abutment in quickly moving water. When retrieved, the boat may look terminal, but it may be possible to force it back into shape. Actually, I have seen several poly kayaks that were deliberately folded in half for shipping purposes, and then used successfully on long trips in remote areas. So before thowing your hands up in despair, try the following.

- Remove any damaged internal fittings if necessary to make the job easier.

- Use the heat from the sun or another source to make the hull more pliable.

- If there are any tears, a small round hole drilled into the end point of the tear may prevent it from continuing.

- Apply weight and force with patience as necessary to return the hull to its original shape.

- Reinstall the internal parts and check for adequate rigidity in the hull, then take it on a trial paddle run.

A final problem that may occur to poly kayaks relates to damage from ultraviolet radiation. *UV deterioration* is a gradual process and is going to be most apparent on older model kayaks that have had a lot of time in the sun. It typically occurs on deck surfaces unless you regularly transport and store the kayak upside down. Look for fading colors and possible networks of small cracks. If the material continues to crack while being flexed, it has reached the end of the line. The only repair options are preventive in nature. Regularly coat exposed deck surfaces with a UV inhibitor, and keep the kayak out of the sun as much as possible.

Composite Hulls

When repairing *composite hulls*—kayaks made from fiberglass, Kevlar, and/or carbon fiber (graphite)—basically follow the same procedures. These cloth-like reinforcing materials are laminated into a composite with one of several resins providing the rigid structural character. The outer surface you see on most composite kayaks is the *gelcoat*, which is basically a thin, hard coat of polyester resin with pigments and added UV inhibitors. This outer protective layer of the kayak is the layer you most likely will be doing basic repairs to.

Structural damage that penetrates the cloth core of the laminate is most easily repaired with patches of fiberglass cloth, which is easier to work with than Kevlar or carbon fiber cloth. If possible, work on the inside of the hull to avoid the irregularity of a raised surface when you are done. The outside can then be touched up with a cosmetic repair. Also avoid doing a thicker job than necessary so that the natural flex of the hull remains consistent at that point.

Gelcoat chip with exposed fiberglass cloth. This type of damage should be repaired ASAP.

WORKING WITH FIBERGLASS-RELATED REPAIR MATERIALS

Working with fiberglass, resins, and related chemicals is serious business. Here are some general tips for doing a good job.

- **Safety.** Always provide adequate ventilation and use rubber or surgical gloves, proper eyewear, and an appropriate respirator when necessary.

- **Organize the work area.** Gather all materials needed including cleanup supplies.

- **Clean and prepare the surface to be repaired.** Remove loose, broken pieces, sand or rough up the contact surface, and clean with alcohol or an appropriate solvent.

- **Work in small manageable doses.** Resins have specific, temperature-dependent *set times*. If working with more than a few ounces or so of the resin, spread it out after mixing in a flat container to reduce heat buildup. While you're at it, have any other small fix-it projects on hand to use up any remaining resin, unless these smaller jobs will distract you from doing a good job on your main task.

- **Smooth out the repaired surface.** As much as possible, smooth out the material before the resin sets to reduce sanding time later. Epoxy, in particular, is difficult to sand. You can trim the resin smooth with a razor blade if you catch the resin as it enters the gel stage. Another option for smoothing the surface is to place a piece of 4- or 6-mil polyethylene plastic over the patched area and smooth the resin through the plastic with a flat object or straightedge. The plastic peels away when the resin is hardened.

- **Use several overlapping layers.** If incorporating fiberglass cloth as part of the repair, overlap layers of progressive sizes to even out the thickness and flex of the patch. Put the largest piece closest to the hull to protect the integrity of its fibers from sanding and further abrasion. Be sure to saturate the cloth thoroughly.

When patching a composite hull, try to match the thickness and stiffness of the patch with those of the hull in the repair section. Whether working on the inside or the outside of the hull, place the largest piece of fiberglass cloth on the damaged area first to protect its fibers from sanding and future abrasion.

- **Choose the right materials.** Although polyester resin is probably adequate for most basic repairs on commercially-made kayaks, it may not adhere well to certain surfaces. Epoxy will stick well but is more expensive. For simple or emergency repairs, the small two-part quick-cure epoxy kits work fine, but for major jobs you will get better results with a good quality kit. Obtain these kits from one of the boating accessory suppliers or one of the professional resin supply sources such as the West System. Epoxy repair kits are also available in putty stick form that works well for small holes or gashes and will cure underwater. If unsure as to what may be best for your particular composite kayak, contact your dealer, the manufacturer, or a knowledgeable boat builder in your area.

GELCOAT AND SURFACE REPAIRS

If the surface abrasion is confined to the gelcoat layer and does not penetrate the interior cloth laminate, it merely requires a cosmetic repair. How meticulous you want to be is a matter of choice; you can leave the surface as is and wait for more serious damage, or on the other end of the scale, you can attempt to restore the hull's glossy, "factory-new" appearance. Scratches that penetrate any measurable amount into the gelcoat leave a telltale, white-colored trail. White and off-white hull colors are the most commonly used, since the scratches don't show as easily.

Many paddlers accept patterns of wear as the kayak ages, allowing these battle scars to tell the stories of past great adventures. Periodic application of a good quality automotive or marine wax will restore some of the factory shine and act to fill in some of the irregularities and keep out grime. A good UV inhibitor does the same. If repairing some area of a waxed hull, however, the wax will need to be thoroughly cleaned off first.

For a bit more of a new look to the gelcoat, work over the surface with a rubbing or polishing compound. If time permits, sand the worn surface with successively finer grades of wet/dry sandpaper, keeping in mind that the gelcoat has a finite thickness. This process also helps restore a brighter look to deck areas faded due to UV exposure.

Actually, filling scratches and nicks with replacement gelcoat becomes a tricky business the older your kayak. Because original colors fade in the sunlight over time, matching this surface with a gelcoat touch-up and creating an invisible repair is difficult at best. White makes the best color match in this endeavor. In order to match the gelcoat, your kayak's manufacturer should be able to determine from your model or serial number records what color mixtures were used.

Gelcoat can be difficult to work with. Here are some helpful points.

- The area to be touched up must be cleaned and prepared carefully. Gelcoat is a variation of polyester resin and may have problems adhering when not done right.

- After mixing, gelcoats tend to be rather runny, making them difficult to contain in the area where wanted. Position the hull as best you can and use tape as a barrier if necessary.

- As the material hardens, it contracts. Another layer may be necessary to achieve perfection. Patience and polishing compound will finish the job.

There are other methods for filling surface dings, as well as deeper cracks and holes, that are somewhat quicker and easier. The general idea is to fill the gap or hole with a durable, waterproof material that will bond solidly with the laminate. Epoxy, automotive patching compound, marine boat repair compound, or polyester or epoxy resin thickened with one of a number of fillers are easier to work with than gelcoat. These fillers provide a more durable fix for deep scratches, chips, and places such as the *stems* (the part of the bow or stern coming up from the keel) where larger chunks have been broken loose.

- Sand and clean thoroughly.

- Use quality materials that are not too old.

- Mix and follow directions carefully.

- Apply an enamel or compatible paint to achieve an approximate color match. Automotive or marine supply dealers should have a good selection of these paints.

FIBERGLASS PATCHING

When you can see fracture lines in the laminate from the inside of the hull or see the daylight through an obvious hole, you will need to make some sort of structural patch. If the spot is accessible from the inside of the kayak, you can do a more aesthetically pleasing job by putting the patch on the inside, allowing a smooth, cosmetic repair on the outside. If not, an outside patch will need to be blended into the surface of the hull as best you can.

Use fiberglass cloth for the reinforcing patch. Kevlar cloth (used for making bulletproof vests) is more expensive, can be extremely difficult to cut to size, and sanding any exposed fibers can be frustrating. The difference in strength for a small patch should not be significant.

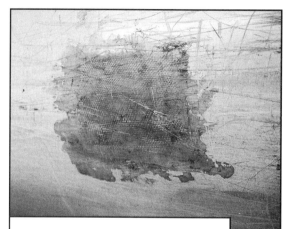

External fiberglass patch on a well-used kayak hull. Place the reinforcing patch on the inside of the hull for a more visually attractive repair and then make a cosmetic repair to the outer gelcoat surface.

Wooden Hulls

Kayaks with wood hulls are generally coated with varnish, paint, or epoxy to seal and protect the wood and to provide an aesthetically appealing appearance. Repairs to these surfaces, whether on a wood strip or plywood hull, will involve resealing and restoring the appearance. These kayaks, like any others, get their share of surface scratches, which should be touched up at least once a season.

If any of these scratches or gouges penetrate the outer protective layer, exposing the wood beneath, it's important to repair them as soon as possible.

The first step in rejuvenating a kayak's surface is to give it a good *(continued on page 56)*

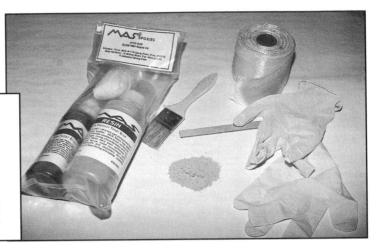

Materials assembled for a wood hull repair: MAS epoxy kit, fiberglass tape, brush, stir stick, wood flour, and latex gloves.
(All photos this page and next by Dale Hedtke)

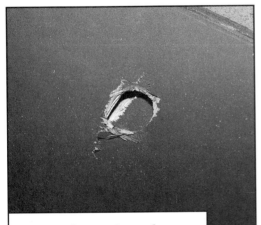

Impact damage in mock-up of plywood hull.

Interior view of damage to plywood.

Damaged piece is trimmed to fit back into place and the edges are coated with epoxy resin.

Fiberglass tape is placed over damaged area and wetted out with epoxy resin. Additional layers of fiberglass cloth can be added later as necessary for reinforcement.

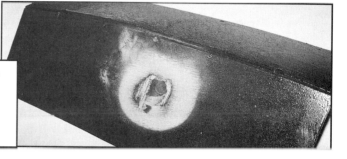

On the outside surface of the hull, the damaged area is sanded and dished in slightly toward the hole.

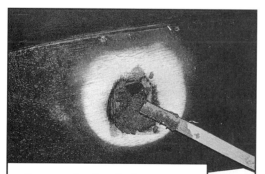

Epoxy mixed with the wood flour is spread into the depression.

The outside repair is smoothed with a putty knife.

The hardened patch has been sanded and painted. A perfect color match may require repainting the whole surface.

(continued from page 53) cleaning and allow the surface to dry thoroughly. Lightly sand the area to be recoated to provide better adhesion. For revarnishing, choose a high quality, exterior grade varnish with UV inhibitors. A high-gloss varnish, I am told, will help reflect sunlight and reduce deterioration over time. For painting or repainting, choose a paint compatible with the existing hull surface. Enamel-based paints adhere to most everything and provide superior protection. Any gouges or nicks that penetrate the epoxy or glass layer into the wood should be filled with a non-absorbent filler or epoxy and sanded smooth before applying the surface coating.

More serious forms of damage are not as common as surface wear and tear, but are usually easily repairable, which is one of the advantages of wood as a boatbuilding material. Investigate separations between strips or panels in the hull or deck to determine their cause. Any internal structural problems should be repaired first, and then the gap can be closed up or filled with epoxy thickened with *wood flour* or another filler that provides a good working consistency. Patch damaged areas using the procedures for fiberglass reconstruction described earlier.

Deck fittings and attached accessories may require periodic repair work. Loose screws can be tightened in several ways. If the wood around the screw hole is sound, either use a waterproof glue or replace with the next larger size screw. A word of caution if using the glue approach: avoid epoxy unless you are certain that you will never need to remove the screw again.

If you own a wood-hull kayak, chances are you either built it yourself or bought it for the aesthetic beauty of wood. The wooden boat community is an extensive and enthusiastic one, and for further ideas and for the camaraderie, make contacts with like-minded paddlers through local clubs, shops, or Internet bulletin boards.

Skin-on-Frame and Folding Kayaks

All kayaks using a flexible skin material will have their own unique set of repairable problems. Abrasion, small holes, tears, and, in the case of canvas, mildew will appear over the course of time. Traditional Inuit skin boats needed constant maintenance. Made of modern materials, your skin craft will go longer between repair sessions, but it is still a more hands-on type of kayak than its solid-hull cousins.

Much of the abrasion occurs along the edges of the supporting framework, especially the keel, stems, and chines. The bow and stern stem areas can get a lot of wear from repeated landings and launchings. Sand and small stones can work their way into the spaces between the hull *stringers* (the thin pieces of wood running the length of the kayak) and fabric, causing bumps that can wear through. Deck and hull surfaces of kayaks that have been stored outside may show fading, cracking, or loss of elasticity from long-term exposure to UV radiation.

Painted canvas hulls require periodic repair work. Small holes against a frame member can be filled with epoxy. Tears may need to be sewn if accessible from the inside or patched with a section of canvas and the appropriate adhesive. Touch up as needed worn sections of canvas or cracking paint, or save these little chores and do a general cleanup once a season. It is not necessary to repaint the entire hull, which of course adds weight to the kayak, unless you are insistent on an exact color match. Consider putting on a preventive patch or *runner* over an area that is showing signs of regular wear.

The urethane- or rubber-coated nylon skins (Hypalon is probably the most common) of folding kayaks can also develop small holes at wear points and cuts from sharp rock and shells. Patching with a piece of the fabric and a urethane adhesive is the standard method of repair. Assemble a repair kit with the proper materials to carry on long outings.

Inflatable Kayaks

Most inflatable hull materials can easily be repaired with a vinyl patching procedure. Individual manufacturers normally offer patch kits as an accessory, or you can do it yourself with vinyl patches and Vynabond. Follow adhesive directions for the best results. Splice long tears in stages using tape to hold the sides of the tear together, and then covering the area with a reinforcing patch. As with skin-on-frame and folding kayaks, carrying a patching repair kit is good insurance.

Polycarbonate Hulls

Another synthetic molded kayak hull material is a *polycarbonate* (used in touring models by Eddyline Kayaks). Called Carbonlite, this material is stiffer and lighter than polyethylene and less expensive than most composites. On the market now for several seasons, it seems to be pretty rugged stuff, resisting scratches and the usual banging around that touring kayaks receive. Because it loses some of its resilience below 0°F (–18°C), polycarb kayaks shouldn't be used or even moved at those low temperatures, not a problem for most paddlers.

Time will tell how big a niche these kayaks will carve into the marketplace, but Carbonlite has interesting potential, as it can be laminated to other materials. It is also easily repairable. Various plastic welding adhesives based on the use of *methyl methacrylate* and related compounds (used in quick-setting household glues) can be used for bonding cracks and for patching. One of these is Devcon Plastic Welder, a two-part adhesive that is commonly available. These adhesives, having a relatively short *cure time*, in the fifteen-minute range, make them ideal for field repairs, but you have to work quickly. Apply fiberglass cloth patches as a reinforcing fabric. After it has cured, the patch can be sanded and painted with an acrylic paint.

Repairs to Components

Although the hull of a kayak takes the majority of abuse from the outside elements, other components of your boat will occasionally need to be fixed or tinkered with to remain in operating order. Whether it's a polyethylene whitewater kayak that can take repeated hard poundings or a hand-crafted skin-on-frame replica that needs regular tweaking, the sooner you deal with minor problems, the less likely you will have major problems at a later date.

Cockpit Coamings and Seats

The outer edges of the coaming on any kayak can get banged up easily during transport, storage, or on the beach. Surface dings and cuts that have ragged or sharp edges should be dealt with in a timely manner to prevent tears or abrasion to the spray skirt. With a good repair kit, you can easily fix these minor problems in the field.

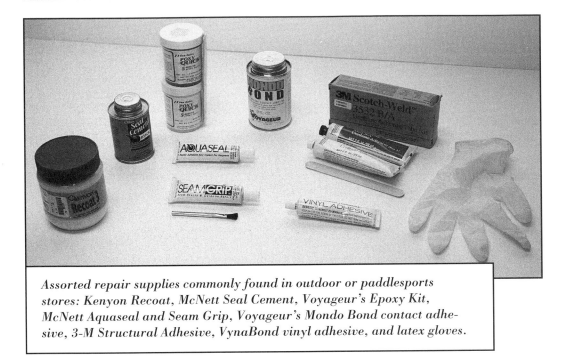

Assorted repair supplies commonly found in outdoor or paddlesports stores: Kenyon Recoat, McNett Seal Cement, Voyageur's Epoxy Kit, McNett Aquaseal and Seam Grip, Voyageur's Mondo Bond contact adhesive, 3-M Structural Adhesive, VynaBond vinyl adhesive, and latex gloves.

Touch up a polyethylene coaming with sandpaper or a small file. Carefully trim burrs that stick up with a sharp knife. If a spray skirt won't stay on snugly and adjusting the skirt with its drawcord doesn't help, rough up the underside of the coaming with a coarse sandpaper to give it more grip. Sanding or filing will smooth out rough spots of fiberglass coamings, and chips or cuts can be filled in with epoxy or covered temporarily in the field with duct tape. Wood of course can be sanded, then sealed with varnish or epoxy.

A more serious repair job is in store if the coaming has broken or is in the process of breaking away from the deck. Polyethylene kayaks have an integral coaming, but other types of kayaks

Assorted adhesives available at hardware, marine, and home-improvement stores: Lexel urethane caulk, Everfix Epoxy Stick, Sportsman's Goop adhesive, and Pliobond adhesive.

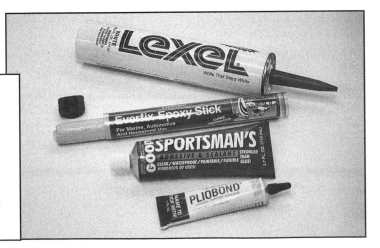

generally have coamings built in by hand. On a composite boat, the coaming, which may be a single unit with a hung seat, can either be fiberglassed into place or bonded in with some sort of adhesive. A glass-reinforced seam is structurally more durable and, if done right, should take all the weight of entries, exits, and lifting. Gaps and cracks can be sealed or patched with a compatible resin. Seal the outside of the seam to prevent water from seeping into the cloth layer. The bonded type of seam is more likely to fail if not done right. It probably would be best to clean up and repair any cracked or broken seam with glass cloth and resin. Take note of the safety precautions discussed earlier when working in the confined space of a cockpit.

Given the wide variety of possible designs of the coaming of a wooden hull or skin-on-frame kayak, it is difficult to generalize about repairs. It may be worth doing some research into new configurations before merely patching up a design that has already failed. Check some of the resources in chapter 8 or contact local clubs and other paddlers or builders for alternative approaches.

Seats

Some of the stock seats installed in commercially made kayaks will require occasional repairs. The fit and comfort of your kayak seat being critical to your paddling performance, you may want to consider upgrading or customizing the seat arrangement before repairing the existing setup. We discuss various options in detail in chapter 5.

The molded plastic seats that come with most kinds of polyethylene kayaks are relatively maintenance-free, and repairs are likely to be limited to keeping them fastened securely in place. Replace any corroding, stripped, or missing bolts to avoid more trouble later. If a plastic seat is cracked or has deteriorated from exposure to sunlight, it probably is not worth trying to fix, other than temporarily with duct tape, and it is time for a factory replacement, or better yet, a customized arrangement. If the edges of the molded seat are causing abrasion spots to appear on the outside of the hull, redistribute the load of these pressure points more widely by experimenting with foam inserts packed inside or around the seat. Use a stiff, crush-resistant, closed-cell foam. Anchor these foam pieces in place with a waterproof contact cement, but be sure of your placements before gluing.

Composite-hull kayaks often come with a molded fiberglass seat that is hung from the cockpit coaming. This arrangement can cause several problems. Stress cracks in the smooth, outer gelcoated surface should be sanded and filled in with putty or resin before they rip the seat of your pants. These hanging seats can also flex sideways, an unwanted and sometimes disconcerting movement, when you are aggressively leaning the kayak to *carve a turn*. Fit closed-cell foam under and on the sides of the seat to prevent this extra flex. Use enough foam to spread out the load on the inside of the hull to avoid abrasion points on the outside.

Hinged seat backs usually have a line running through a cleat to control the tilt of the backrest. Though convenient and comfortable, the line is subject to abrasion where it runs around a corner, especially in fiberglass. If it's wearing through, replace this line before it breaks on a trip, and consider reinforcing the line by running it through a length of flexible plastic tubing. A similar problem can occur with the webbing of a padded back band if it is mounted through a slot cut in a fiberglass or plastic seat support. An abrasive edge like this can be padded with a small section of plastic tubing cut to length, split along one side, and inserted over the edge of the slot.

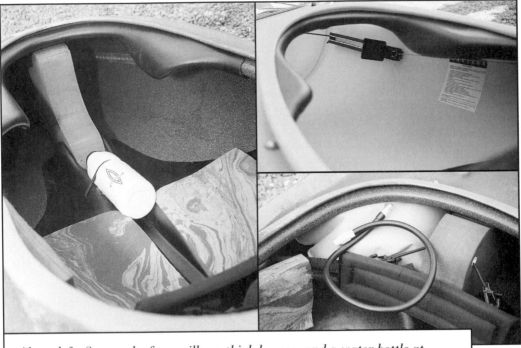

Above left: *Seat pads, foam pillars, thigh braces, and a water bottle attachment of a whitewater kayak.* Top right: *Interior view of a touring kayak showing the thigh braces, adjustable footrest, and the front bulkhead.* Above right: *Hip pads, back band, rear pillar, and flotation of a whitewater kayak are visible in the cockpit.*

Bulkheads and Internal Parts

Whitewater kayaks and some touring kayaks are outfitted with foam or plastic pillars to provide the hull structural rigidity. These pillars are usually held in place by bolts or by being wedged into position by other parts, such as the seat assembly or a *thigh-brace panel*, usually a trouble-free configuration. If you are doing repairs or modifications to these other parts, be sure that the pillars remain firmly in place.

Bulkheads in touring and sea kayaks create compartments in the bow and stern as well as provide flotation. As such, they must be sealed to prevent leaking, and that leads to occasional repairs. Bulkheads installed in commercially made composite kayaks are generally free of problems. In the event of a leak or delamination, a urethane structural adhesive can be used on a foam bulkhead, and a compatible resin or epoxy can be used on a fiberglass one. Again, take precautions when working with these adhesives in a confined space.

Getting bulkheads to stay sealed in a polyethylene kayak is a different matter. Particularly with older poly kayaks, the silicone caulking compounds provide only a temporary seal that needs to be touched up after a period of use. More recent manufacturing methods, including the use of plastic welding techniques, are more secure. Try Lexel polyurethane caulk, which will provide a better seal than a silicone-based sealant.

The internal frameworks of wooden, skin-on-frame, and folding kayaks have a host of different repair issues. Plywood and strip-built kayak bulkheads may require occasional attention. Skin-on-frame and folding kayaks derive their shape and strength from the internal frame. This structure is inherently more flexible than a rigid-hull kayak, which gives the individual pieces some cushioning from impacts and extreme stresses. Nevertheless, if you do get a cracked, broken, or bent frame member, repair it as soon as you can. Unless the break has punctured the hull fabric or threatens to do so, the kayak will probably still paddle all right to get you back home or to a secure place to do at least a temporary repair.

Folding kayaks obviously offer an advantage in terms of accessibility to the interior frame parts. Repairs to the farther recesses of a skin-on-frame kayak may have to wait until you can open up the skin fabric in the workshop. You can improvise temporary to semi-permanent repairs to broken members using duct tape or by splicing in a section of wood or tubing of a similar length and tying, taping, or gluing it into place. Some folding kayaks come with a spare frame member that can be used for this purpose. For a completely permanent, duplicate replacement of a broken part, it is best to go to the original manufacturer if possible. If building your own frame kayak, save or make a selection of frame pieces to have on hand for easy repair work later.

Deck Accoutrements

Most deck-mounted accessories fall into the domain of touring and sea kayaks, but all kayaks have some kind of grab loops or toggles built into the bow and stern of the boat. These facilitate the carrying of the kayak to and from the water and serve as an important safety accessory, providing a handhold for rescuing a paddler in the water, as well as a useful place for holding onto the kayak while in the water and to hook up a towline. For those reasons, the grab loops should be long enough to allow a good grip from a variety of angles without trapping or pinching fingers.

If the line used in the grab loop is getting frayed, don't delay replacing it. Much of the wear and tear on the loops can come from their use as a tie-down point while cartopping. If your grab loop has a toggle handle with a knot on the inside, work the knot out so that you can see how it was tied, and then remove the old line. Measure the length and add a few more inches if you want more length to the loops. Replace with new line and reverse the procedure, working the knot back into position.

A good quality polypropylene line is best for the grab loops and other deck lines because it is light and resists stretching. Nylfloat, an abrasion-resistant polypropylene line with a braided nylon sheath available from Voyageur, is a durable alternative for many uses. Spectra cord is another extremely durable but expensive line that is often used in throw bags and will make bombproof grab loops. It is often available at outdoor stores that carry climbing equipment. *Shock cord,*

Grab handle showing one of the inside knots.

used on the decks of touring kayaks, comes in several diameters, with the thicker, ¼ inch obviously being stiffer and more durable. It is sometimes hard to keep a good knot tied in shock cord, so plan on using some electrical tape or perhaps an adhesive to keep the knot tight and secure.

Hatches

As discussed in chapter 3, some deck hatch systems will leak a bit no matter what you do with them, and others will give you years of dry security. Round and oval VCP (Valley Canoe Products) and VCP-style rubber hatches are quite watertight and will require little maintenance. I have heard periodic stories about this type of hatch cover popping off when the kayak heats in the sun, particularly when the kayak is being transported, but I suspect this is relatively rare. One solution for this problem is to drill a small pressure release hole in the bulkhead to allow expanding air to escape into the cockpit.

You may be suspicious of drilling a hole into a bulkhead and rightly so. However, if this hole is kept to ¹⁄₁₆ inch or less and positioned approximately in the middle of the bulkhead, halfway between the deck and the hull, the kayak cockpit would have to be half filled with water before the hole would be exposed to water, and the amount of water that could trickle in during the time of a typical rescue would be fairly minute.

Chronic leaks around large hatches may be more difficult to correct. Larger perimeters are harder to keep sealed, particularly if there are curvatures built into the hatch opening or cover. As the hull and deck flex slightly while moving through the waves, water can make its way in past gaskets. Compressed, torn, or worn-out gaskets may need to be replaced. Attempts at patching and splicing may create differentially stiffer sections, which can continue to let seeping water past. If possible, check with the manufacturer of your kayak to see if there are any replacement gaskets or newer types of gasket material and other techniques to reseal their hatch systems. Otherwise, you are on your own, and a replacement can be made with closed-cell foam, using the old gasket as a template. Remove the old foam and adhesive residue completely and use waterproof contact cement to install the new gasket. Neoprene covers used on some hatches can be repaired in a similar manner as neoprene spray skirts, discussed later in this chapter.

A camming-style hatch cover from Eddyline. In general, the larger and more rigid a hatch cover is, the more difficult it is to keep totally watertight.

Field repairs to broken or leaky hatches will rely on your trusty roll of duct tape. If leaking is going to cause a potentially serious problem in rough water conditions, you can seal the entire hatch shut with the tape to get to where you need to go. Just pack your kayak so that nothing you will soon need is in that compartment. In the event of a lost hatch cover, enough duct tape and a piece of polyethylene plastic or Mylar emergency-blanket material makes a serviceable temporary cover.

Rudders and Skegs

Rudder and skeg systems probably generate as many adjustments and repairs as any other piece of kayak equipment. Assuming you have kept up with basic maintenance, such as replacing lines and cables as they age, most repairs involve damage that occurs while paddling. The most likely source of that damage occurs in the shore zone as you come in for a landing and forget that the rudder or skeg is deployed. Paddling backward with the rudder down, landing hard with a breaking wave, or broaching to the waves at the shore can put a lot of stress on the rudder or skeg blade, possibly bending or breaking it. The obvious solution is not to leave it down, but we all forget once in a while.

Aluminum blades can be bent back into shape, but there is a limit how much of this they will take. A broken blade is difficult to repair or replace in the field, unless you are carrying a spare for this relatively unlikely eventuality. If you find the broken half, a splint with a thin strip of wood or metal could be anchored with duct tape. In most situations, it would be more practical to paddle home without it and replace it later.

Unless carrying the appropriate spare parts and the tools to work with them, repairs to other rudder parts are difficult in the field. Some of these parts can be obtained from the manufacturer and carried in a repair kit.

Skeg housings can occasionally jam with beach pebbles upon launching and landing, so check the operation of the blade after launching from those sorts of beaches to verify that it drops out freely. If a stone is really wedged into the housing, take care when prying it out to prevent marring the edge of the hull. With skeg mechanisms, the working parts are largely contained on the inside of the kayak. This protects them from outside damage but makes them more difficult to access for possible repairs.

Accessories

Just as important as keeping your boat afloat, key paddling accessories must be kept in good working order, or you won't be getting far. This section explains how to repair these items.

Paddles

Paddles are most commonly damaged along the tips of the blades. If you touch up minor problems regularly, you can avoid more major projects later. Small chips and dents along the edges of virtually any type of blade can be sanded to smooth them out. Use a medium and then a finer grit sandpaper if you want to be meticulous. On many types of molded plastic blades, this is all

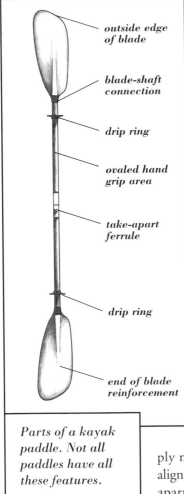

outside edge
of blade

blade-shaft
connection

drip ring

ovaled hand
grip area

take-apart
ferrule

drip ring

end of blade
reinforcement

*Parts of a kayak
paddle. Not all
paddles have all
these features.*

you need to do. On a composite paddle (cloth and resin), you can also dab on or paint a thin coat of epoxy to act as additional protection. Check for any signs of delamination and fill with epoxy as necessary. A crack of any length may need reinforcing with a fiberglass patch, but don't overdo it as you will be adding weight to the blade. If you are unsure about the composition of the paddle blades, seek advice from a paddlesports shop or from the paddle manufacturer.

Varnish the sanded edges of a wooden paddle with a waterproof varnish. Fix small splits or delaminations by working some waterproof wood glue into the split. Carefully flexing the wood at that point will help the glue to move into the split. Allow to dry, and then sand and varnish. A more serious split may require a fiberglass reinforcing patch, but again keep in mind that such repairs add weight to the blade. Otherwise, glue as best you can and position some clamps and blocks of wood to hold the crack closed while the glue dries.

Cracking can also occur at the end of the reinforcing rib that tapers in from the blade's shaft. This area may have differing flex patterns, and if the blade is overflexed, such as while pushing off during a launch, stress cracks could develop at this point. A bad enough crack will require patching and perhaps relegating the paddle to spare status.

Many varieties of synthetic paddle blades are fitted and bonded into the hollow shaft. If a blade comes loose, it simply needs to be reglued, taking into account the proper angle of alignment in relation to the other blade or to the position of the take-apart joint. Sand and clean the old glued surfaces to get a better bond. Urethane structural adhesive or epoxy works in most cases.

The shaft of a take-apart paddle will have a joint or ferrule that may require some attention. Although these joints are a convenience, with age they tend to get looser as the inner and outer sides of the ferrule wear against each other. This sloppiness on a fiberglass ferrule can be easily eliminated with the following method.

- Sand and clean the surface of the smaller (male) half.

- The next time you are doing an epoxy repair, save a dab and smear a bit (go very easy on the quantity) around on the surface of the ferrule.

- Allow to dry completely. (You are trying to increase the circumference of the inside ferrule slightly.)

- Try the two halves together after the epoxy is completely cured and sand as needed to gain a tight and even fit.

A loose metal ferrule can be fixed by giving the outer half a small and careful tweak in a vise to crimp the diameter and tighten it up.

Another occasional problem is water that gets into a hollow shaft somehow. The faint sloshing of water while paddling is a real nuisance, not to mention the extra weight. The water could be getting in through an incomplete seal at the base of the blade or possibly past a plug in the shaft near the take-apart joint. Getting this water back out can be a bit of a problem. It may be easiest to try to remove or drill through the plug in the end. In a one-piece paddle, you may need to try to twist one of the blades off, or if they don't want to budge, drill a small hole into the base of the shaft for a temporary drain. Then search for the leak's source and seal accordingly.

All this talk of problems with synthetic paddles may have you longing for the simplicity of wood. Although not subject to many of the preceding problems, a good wood paddle is more likely to be a victim of serious breakage during rescues, landings, and so on. A partial or complete break in a shaft or blade is going to necessitate some creative fiberglass work or woodworking skills beyond most paddlers' expertise. Wood is a very repairable material, so don't give up hope for your favorite paddle. Most wood paddle manufacturers probably offer some kind of repair services or can give a referral.

Spray Skirts

In the long run, most spray skirts and other fabric-based gear will succumb to the effects of UV deterioration. This effect is cumulative and irreversible, and my experience has been that these pieces of gear will go about ten years before reaching the end of their usefulness when serious fading and shredding sets in. This is an approximation; people in the more southern latitudes may see much faster degradation. Use of fabric conditioners with UV protection as preventive maintenance is well worth the effort for extending the value of your equipment.

Other problems are more repairable. Tears and splitting seams are relatively easy to sew, patch, or seal. Good quality nylon skirts are made with heavy-duty seams and taped to become watertight, but occasionally leak. Factory heat-bonded seam tapes are not easily resealed with home equipment, but use of a seam sealer like Seam Grip will stop the leaks. Splitting seams can be re-sewn by hand, and then sealed with Seam Grip for a serviceable repair. Some manufacturers may warrant their seam construction, so it may be worth a call to your local paddleshop or distributor if your skirt is relatively new.

If a seam at an edge of the nylon fabric is in danger of unraveling because of fraying, you can sometimes seal the fabric edge with a heat source to stop this process. Otherwise, just touch it up with seam cement. The seam on the perimeter of the skirt that forms the channel for the shock cord is often subject to this problem as a result of the tension put on that seam.

Skirts utilizing a combination of neoprene and nylon are becoming more popular. The neoprene *deck* provides a secure cockpit fit and good drainage, and the nylon *tube* allows adjustability and comfort for the wearer. The seam between the neoprene and the nylon is a critical one to keep from leaking. Aquaseal should work in most cases to keep this seam in good condition.

You may have to search for the source of some leaks. Major seams may be seam taped, but pockets in the waist tube or even a sewn-on logo may not be. Solve these problems with a thin bead of seam cement. The idea is to get the glue into the stitch holes created by the sewing process. Seam glues work best if you don't put too much on; a thin layer will adhere longer.

Occasionally, the urethane coatings that make nylon waterproof will deteriorate from prolonged exposure to moisture, mildew, and other factors and will begin to flake away. This is a fairly terminal condition, though you can extend the fabric's life by recoating the fabric with such products as Kenyon's Recoat 3 or Nikwax's Tent and Gear Proof. These products coat the nylon with a waterproof layer, but they never last as long as the original fabric mill's urethane coating. Follow the directions on these products closely for best results.

Neoprene skirts can be a bit easier to repair than nylon ones. A urethane-based neoprene cement such as Aquaseal can be used to solve a host of different problems. An optional *accelerating catalyst* is available with these cements to speed the cure time. You can reseal split seams and tears by spreading the fabric out flat and making sure the cement works down into the split. Longer tears can be taped shut at intervals and glued in stages. Lightly coat with urethane adhesive those areas of abrasion or deterioration to retard further damage. Also, if you have a skirt that has trouble staying on a slippery polyethylene cockpit coaming, put a bead of urethane adhesive around the skirt's inside perimeter where it contacts the rim so that it grips more securely. Though flexible, the adhesive is not as stretchy as the neoprene fabric, so it is best not to coat too great an area of the fabric that needs to stretch.

The built-in *shock cord*, which provides tension on the coaming, most likely will last the life of the skirt with no further maintenance. If, however, the shock cord breaks or loses its stretchiness, you may need to replace it. Before pulling the old one out of the skirt, attach the replacement to the end of the original with some duct tape. When you remove the old cord, the new one should come through with ease.

Flotation Bags and Dry Bags

Using flotation and waterproof storage bags is an integral part of the sport of kayaking, and keeping them serviceable is an ongoing maintenance task. We touched on basic repairs of small leaks in chapter 3, but now we'll look at various repair issues in more detail.

You can usually obtain complete kits for repairing float bags and dry bags from the manufacturers of those bags, or you can patch equipment using an adhesive and cut pieces of vinyl or nylon fabrics. The basic repair material for float bags, storage bags, paddle floats, map cases, and other items made of vinyl is Vynabond or some similar vinyl adhesive. You can dab this vinyl cureall on small leaks or cuts, or you can apply it as an adhesive bond to patches that are covering larger holes and tears. For various coated or laminated nylon fabrics, as well as neoprene, use a urethane adhesive for reinforcing and patching. Cotol, a curing accelerator, when used with Aquaseal helps to complete the repairing process in a matter of a few hours.

Other parts of bags can be repaired or replaced as well. Surface areas that seem to get regular abrasion can be coated with Aquaseal as a protective layer. It is unlikely you will have trouble with the plastic buckles on various brands of dry bags, but if you do, replacements are readily available at well-stocked outdoor equipment stores and mail-order sources. Since most of these parts are permanently fastened into place, you will have to improvise a splice with fabric and adhesive. Replacement valve kits are available from Voyageur and probably other dry bag makers. If in a cre-

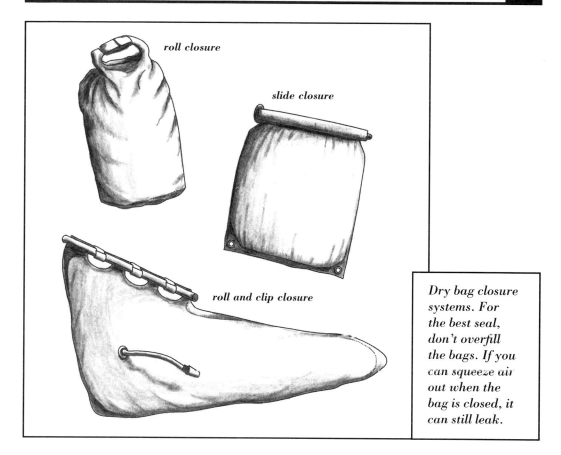

roll closure

slide closure

roll and clip closure

Dry bag closure systems. For the best seal, don't overfill the bags. If you can squeeze air out when the bag is closed, it can still leak.

ative mood, you can cannibalize air hoses from old, retired flotation bags for use on another bag. Just cut the hose out, leaving a radius of an inch or so of material around the base of the hose.

While doing these repairs, don't overlook hunting for the cause of some of these leaks. Look inside the kayak for sharp edges, exposed bolts, or hidden debris that could wear away at fabric. Exposed bolts from deck-mounted accessories are a common culprit, and these can be trimmed down carefully with a hacksaw blade or buffered with a glued-on piece of foam.

Renewing Clothing

As discussed in chapter 3, keeping your paddling garments dry and clean is half the battle of proper maintenance and getting the most out of your investment in comfort and safety. As a start, provide your fabric gear with a place to hang and dry freely, and get into the habit of washing things regularly to reduce the possibility of mildew damage.

Use a brand of outdoor gear cleaner that is biodegradable, nondetergent, quicker to rinse out, and easy on existing water-repellent coatings. Some of the better ones are Tech Wash from Nikwax, Granger's G-Clean, and Tectron Pro Wash. You can apply the cleaner to small areas as a spot remover before washing. For best results, follow directions on both the cleaner and the garment's care instruction tag.

Other fabric-care products fall roughly into three categories. The first group, water-repellency sprays and wash-in treatments, produces a somewhat temporary coating that causes water to bead up and run off. Silicone sprays tend to wear out after a few washings. Nikwax offers several products directed at specific types of fabrics, including CottonProof for cotton, canvas, and cotton-polyester blends, and PolarProof for fleece or synthetic pile, wool, and nylon outerwear. DWR (durable water repellency) treatments, such as Tectron DWR Water Repellent Spray or Wash-In, can also be used on the nylon side of coated fabrics to retard soiling and reduce the fabric's tendency to absorb water. The Tectron DWR also contains a UV screening agent, which makes it useful on exposed fabrics like PFDs and spray skirts.

The second group of care products renews the waterproofness of coated nylon fabrics, which can include paddle garments, but is also useful for nylon spray skirts, cockpit covers, tarps, and so on. These coatings, generally a urethane applied by the fabric manufacturer, can deteriorate and begin to flake off due to age, contact with petrochemicals, UV radiation, or long-term exposure to moisture and mildew. It is impossible to repair this type of damage to nylon gear permanently, but these treatments buy you time. Kenyon's Recoat 3 and WaterShed from Nikwax are waterbased, nonaerosol products that do this job.

The third major category of products are the DWR treated fabrics, including the market leader Gore-Tex. Durable water repellency refers to a fluoropolymer-based finish put on *waterproof-breathable* (W-B) fabrics by the manufacturers to allow water to bead up and run off. The laminated or coated construction and microporous structure of these W-B fabrics allow water vapor from the humid environment inside the garment to escape. This reduces sweat buildup, resulting in a more comfortable garment to wear over a longer time period. The tiny size of the fabric's pores prevents water, with its surface-tension properties, from seeping through from the outside. The DWR finish prevents the outer layer of nylon from absorbing water, or *wetting out*, and effectively blocking the route of the escaping water vapor from the inside.

This wetting-out factor can lead to a feeling of dampness or even to condensation that may be mistaken for leakage in the fabric. Your skin cannot easily distinguish between being cool and being wet, and this adds to the assumption that the W-B fabric is not

Water beads on coated nylon or Gore-Tex fabric garments properly treated with water-repellency chemicals. This prevents the fabric from getting saturated and, in the case of waterproof-breathable fabrics, allows breathability to be maintained.

working. If you are paddling hard and sweating, you will also be exceeding the fabric's short-term ability to move water vapor through. Dirt, soap residue, and even campfire smoke can also retard the ability of the DWR to do its job. Fortunately, the effectiveness of the DWR can be renewed for a period of time by washing the garment and rinsing thoroughly to remove these impurities. In the case of Gore-Tex, W. L. Gore, the fabric manufacturer, recommends tumble drying the garment on a medium heat setting for 50 minutes after washing. This heat process revives the bonds of the DWR to the fabric. If you are working with one of the coated W-B fabric garments, check that manufacturer's recommendations.

This DWR factory finish will last through several seasons and many washings and renewals, but will eventually wear out, thus leading to the aftermarket DWR treatment products. The most durable of these are compounds with a fluoropolymer base that bonds more completely with the fabric threads than a silicon spray. Such products as TX-Direct from Nikwax, Tectron DWR Water Repellent, Granger's Superpruf, and Scotchguard from 3M all fit in this category. Some of these require machine washing and others are a spray-on. The wash-in versions are probably the most effective, since they will penetrate deeper and distribute more evenly. Follow directions carefully when using these technical products.

For Gore-Tex fabrics, W. L. Gore has introduced a DWR treatment called Revivex. This one works as a spray-on while the garment is still wet from a wash cycle. The treated garment is then run through a 50-minute dry cycle on medium heat to set the DWR polymer. The company also emphasizes that the key ingredient for proper maintenance is to keep your gear clean.

A certain amount of confusion about the efficiency of waterproof-breathable fabrics comes from their use in saltwater conditions. The salt residues on a W-B fabric, like the dirt and pollutants mentioned above, are *hydrophilic*, attracting moisture and causing a similar "wetting-out" effect. This leads to clamminess and condensation and the sensation that the garment may be leaking.

The answer to this is to keep the garment rinsed off with freshwater after every use and follow the washing and drying instructions as previously discussed. On a long trip in remote areas, a heavily salt-encrusted jacket can even be rinsed in salt water if necessary to remove most of it. I have done several long saltwater trips, including in Alaska, with Gore-Tex products, and had no problems with fabric functioning as intended. Salt water can compromise some W-B fabrics with coatings and some earlier renditions of Gore-Tex fabrics, but I believe these issues have been resolved. It is important to understand the physics of W-B fabrics and their limitations before assessing their functionality. There is no way for anyone to stay totally dry in a water environment, and these "miracle fabrics" are only another tool in this quest to keep as dry as possible.

FABRIC

Technical paddle clothing will need care and occasional repairs. You can patch small holes and tears in nylon or neoprene fabrics while in the field with duct tape or fabric repair tape. Products such as Kenyon's Repair Tape, McNett's Iron Mend for neoprene, and Gore-Tex Repair Kits work in this situation. These patches can last a long time and will certainly get you home from even a long trip, at which time you can do a more permanent and aesthetically pleasing repair. Many garments will come with a fabric swatch, and it is a good idea to save these if you think you will ever want to do a matching patch. Any sewn seams on a patch or waterproof outerwear will need to be seam sealed. *Seam taping* as is done by the manufacturers is beyond the realm of do-it-yourself repairs, so you may want to consider checking out the garment maker's policies on repairing their products. Making repairs to Gore-Tex laminates is also a technical process and might best be sent to one of several Gore-authorized repair service centers.

Occasionally, zippers will need repair or replacement. A zipper that separates periodically may just need a new slider. A replacement zipper can sometimes be sewn to the backing material of the old zipper, thus avoiding the process of tearing out a seam in the fabric. You can clean and revitalize these hard-working parts with zipper care products such as Zip Tech from McNett.

Latex seals in paddle jackets and dry suits are especially vulnerable to chemical and UV deterioration and sharp objects. Even with the best of care, they will not last the life of the rest of the garment. Treat seals regularly with 303 Protectant. It soon will be time for replacing seals when the latex loses its suppleness or turns a grayish color. Replacement kits are available from some paddlesports shops or can be obtained from the garment manufacturer. Although doable, the replacement process can be rather tedious. Manufacturers and independent outdoor gear repair centers will do this work if you prefer.

Neoprene wetsuits and other garments will eventually get torn and abraded, but neoprene is a lot easier to patch than nylon fabrics, which require sewing. You can readily fill or splice tears and holes in neoprene with Aquaseal or other rubber cements. Follow directions for the particular adhesive; some products may work better if both sides of a tear are coated with the glue. Long tears can be bonded in stages, with sections being held together temporarily by tape. Use a piece of polyethylene plastic or wax paper to help smooth the adhesive out without making a mess. Go easy on the amount of adhesive used; reinforcing patches and splices may retard the fabric's ability to stretch, and if they are located on the back or seat of the wetsuit, you may be able to feel the repair when you are in a sitting position. Iron Mend, from McNett, another alternative for worn or torn areas, is an iron-on fabric patching material that can cover tears and add abrasion resistance.

Fleece-lined, midweight stretch Lycra or "fuzzy rubber" garments are increasing in popularity for virtually all spectrums of kayaking. Designed for exposure to moderately cold water, but also for comfort and flexibility, this fabric is available from most paddlesports clothing manufacturers. Aquatec, Splash Gear, and Rapidstyle are some of the popular brands. Tears in this family of fabrics can be stitched or treated like neoprene and patched with Aquaseal. Iron Mend will work on these fabrics as well. Some of the earlier renditions of this fabric may have had a delamination problem in high-pressure wear areas such as the seat.

Kayaking footwear receives a lot of abrasion while being squeezed in and out of cramped cockpits, shuffled around on rocky beaches, and used wet for long periods of time. Delaminations and worn heels and toes can be bonded or coated with Aquaseal, Freesole, Barge cement, or similar flexible urethane adhesives. Some of these adhesives cure by pulling water vapor from the air, so cure times can be reduced by placing the footwear in a humid location.

UV degradation is potentially a concern for any paddle outerwear that may get regular exposure to the summer sun. This is especially true of PFDs and spray skirts, but your favorite jacket or hat can be affected as well. Extend the life of these key pieces of equipment by using 303 Protectant or Tectron Water Repellent with sunscreen additives; apply as directed.

Emergency Gear

Periodically check the rope components of rescue throw ropes and towlines for any damage that might compromise their strength. Rinse or wash lines that have been dragged in the dirt or sand of a shoreline to prevent small abrasive particles from getting at their core. If the rope has been used in a *Z-pulley setup* or any other procedure to extract a pinned kayak or canoe, it may be time to consider retiring it.

Compasses

Of all the nifty gadgets and electronic devices you can carry on a kayak touring outing, your compass is the most important. But do you know how accurate it is? To give it a checkup, first make sure the *compass mechanism*—a rotating needle, wheel, or dome—turns freely inside its housing through all 360 degrees of direction. In the case of a deck compass that isn't easily removable from the kayak, you'll have to do this in your kayak on the water (an excuse to go for a paddle) or by rotating the kayak around on a lawn. Then make sure you don't have any steel bolts or other magnet-attracting metals in the vicinity of the compass. Twelve inches or so should do it unless you're carrying an anvil. Use the compass itself or another household magnet to check bolts and other items if you are not sure of their composition.

Next, check the compass against a known bearing. One way to do this is to go to a location where you can get an accurate fix on a landmark with a map. Compare this bearing with the reading from the compass, after correcting for the magnetic declination in that location. Another option if you own several compasses is to compare them all. If they all essentially agree, then you can assume the best. If you get different readings, try another method unless you want to do some process of elimination. My preferred compass check method is to utilize the North Pole Star, which for this purpose can be assumed to be due north. On a clear night wherever you are in the northern hemisphere, you can visually determine some due north landmark to which to compare the compass, again correcting for declination. You can note the landmark for morning or use a flashlight to read the compass.

Some marine compasses have adjustment screws for correcting the compass mechanism. This process can be tricky, so follow directions carefully. If your compass has a consistent error, you can either learn to compensate for it, or replace it. For most recreational navigation work, an error of several degrees or more is still within the accuracy needed. Just be aware of this and plan accordingly.

If you do paddling excursions in areas of widely different latitudes, your compass may be affected by *magnetic inclination*. The earth's magnetic lines tend to angle up in the equatorial regions, then out and down in the polar regions. This angling causes most compasses, which are balanced for a certain range of latitude, to tilt one way or the other when used in different parts of the world. If the compass mechanism still rotates freely, it is usable. Most compass manufacturers can supply compasses balanced for different parts of the world if needed.

The final consideration on compasses is one to heed when packing the kayak. Take care not to pack gear with metal, such as cameras and stainless-steel cookware, in the immediate vicinity of the compass, especially if the compass is mounted well forward on the deck above the bow compartment. The larger or more dense the metal object, the farther you should stash it from the compass. You don't want to be several miles into a fog crossing, only to discover you have been following your Dutch oven.

Electronic Gadgets

Complex instruments that use batteries and water, especially salt water, are an uneasy combination. Use good quality cameras, radios, and GPS navigation devices in a water environment diligently and with care, or they can be quickly trashed. It is true that many of these devices are available in a "waterproof" or "water-resistant" construction, but I have heard enough horror stories from fellow paddlers about gadget failures in the field to know one should take these claims with a bit of caution.

Here are some general thoughts about the use of these instruments. First, come to a clear understanding of what any manufacturer's claims of waterproofness really mean. Find out if the item is truly immersion-proof to a certain depth, or just splash resistant. Find out if certain parts are excluded from these claims. Be sure to determine how much and for how long the warranty on the product covers. And if you can, research how the given manufacturer or distributor stands behind these claims. A strong warranty won't help you if the gadget dies in the field, but it's nice to know that it will eventually be fixed or replaced.

Next, protect your gear as much as possible with waterproof bags or containers. Sand, dirt, and water pollution can take their toll, even of totally waterproof items. With a little thought and practice, you can develop a storage system that will protect your valuable gear, yet allow it to be reasonably accessible. And finally, keep these things clean and dry. Rinse salt water off at every opportunity—you can even carry a little extra freshwater for this purpose on a short trip. A small, clean cotton towel is also handy. Pay particular attention to keeping battery compartments cleaned out and free of sand on the seals.

As a photography enthusiast, I have accumulated an extensive photo collection by taking along a relatively expensive 35-mm camera on many outings, paddling thousands of miles on long trips in both fresh- and salt water. In the process, I have lost only one camera, a small point-and-shoot that went fifteen years before its final dousing. These electronic gadgets can add a lot to our enjoyment—and safety, in the case of marine-band radios—while kayaking. With some care and advance planning, you should be able to get a reasonable lifespan out of these pieces of gear.

Repairs in the Field

Sooner or later on a paddle trip of any length, you may be confronted with the need to fix something before you can proceed. A leak in the kayak is the most obvious example, but a broken paddle, a torn jacket, and many other accidents can happen. In most cases, field repairs should be considered temporary measures, mostly directed at getting you back to the *takeout*. Unless you have a very complete repair kit, lots of spare time, and ideal working conditions, it will be much easier to do the repair right when you are back at home.

Almost any repair in the field revolves around the ubiquitous roll of duct tape. Armed with this multipurpose material, you can patch a leak, splint a broken paddle, stop a rip from spreading, or even make an emergency back band. My rule of thumb would be that if you can't fix a piece

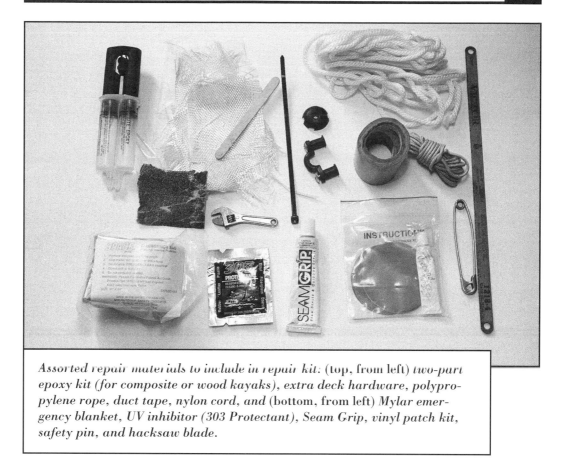

Assorted repair materials to include in repair kit: (top, from left) two-part epoxy kit (for composite or wood kayaks), extra deck hardware, polypropylene rope, duct tape, nylon cord, and (bottom, from left) Mylar emergency blanket, UV inhibitor (303 Protectant), Seam Grip, vinyl patch kit, safety pin, and hacksaw blade.

of equipment such as a compass or flashlight, consider bringing a spare. An absolutely essential item like a paddle also calls for a spare, at least one in every group.

Duct tape isn't the only thing you need in your repair kit. The nature and length of the trip, the size of the group, and the distance from help along the route will have a bearing on your list. Many of the following items can be shared within a group to cut down on duplication.

- Patching materials for hull repair. For that long trip in a remote location, bring a basic fiberglass patching kit, including a two-part epoxy resin, some cloth, small scissors to trim the cloth, mixing stick and tray, and latex or nitrile gloves. For fabric hulls, bring a swatch of the fabric and a compatible adhesive.

- Spare parts for key pieces of equipment. These can include extra deck pad eyes, stainless steel bolts and nuts, rudder parts, cables, drain plug, frame section, and so on. Tools necessary to fit these parts need to be included. A pocket multipurpose tool is great but ineffective if you have a part that requires a screwdriver and a pliers at the same time.

- Sewing kit with fabric tape.

- Aquaseal and/or other repair adhesives to match the gear you are using.

- Nylon cord, ⅛-inch, about 50 feet, has almost as many potential fix-it and camp uses as duct tape.

- Matches or a butane lighter. Good to have these stashed in several locations.

- Several heavy-duty plastic bags.

- Length of stretch cord or several bungee cords.

- Other useful items may include a short hacksaw blade, small section of minicell foam, some corrosion-proof wire, and a Mylar emergency blanket.

- Camping and other gear parts and repair kit, for stoves, etc.

5

CUSTOMIZING YOUR BOAT

Kayaking in all its aspects is a sport of physical and mental dexterity. A kayaker meets the challenges of the earth's surface water in one form or another using a variation of a simple craft that dates back thousands of years. Over the millennia, the Inuit undoubtedly tinkered with their boats and water gear, exchanging information with others near and far, to make these tools work for them in their harsh, changing environment. Today, as recreational kayakers, we too gain satisfaction from tinkering with our boats and gear, customizing our kayaks and accessorizing with the proper gear to make them meet our specific paddling needs.

Unless you build your own kayak from scratch, you will need to do some modifications to any stock boat to make it work for your intended purpose. The interrelated factors of fit, performance, convenience, and safety dictate our customizing needs.

The most important factor is fit, since it relates closely to performance and safety. Making the kayak fit our individual bodies is as important for appropriate control and comfort as it is to fit a

Much of the emphasis on customizing a kayak will center on outfitting the seat and the thigh and back supports in the kayak cockpit.

bicycle or a pair of skis properly. Performance relates to the way the kayak and paddle do the things we must do to navigate through the water. For convenience, we want certain things available when we need them as we paddle. And for safety's sake, we want the configuration of kayak and gear to add to our margin of error, making it more likely we will return without mishap.

This customizing process is a constantly evolving one. Almost all aspects of kayaking are undergoing a dynamic level of change and innovation, and our individual needs and goals will evolve with these changes. Many of us who have paddled for years may wonder how we made do with the skills and the gear that seemed so hot back then. Yet, the basics never change. It's not the gear, but what we do with the gear that counts.

Outfitting the Cockpit

Cockpit fit is the key to paddling performance. The adage that you "wear" your whitewater kayak is true for all kayaks as well. Kayak propulsion takes more than just sitting and moving our arms back and forth. Efficient paddling technique involves the shoulders and most of the muscles of the torso, so your upper body needs to be free to reach, turn, and flex. As you paddle, you are pulling yourself forward, and you must be firmly seated and bracing with your feet to prevent sliding farther forward into the kayak. As you encounter progressively difficult conditions—whether you seek them out or not—you will need to lean, brace, and sweep, which requires your hips, lower back, and thighs to be holding the boat.

These points of contact with the kayak are where the energy you put into the paddle forces the kayak to go where you want it to, and thus are the focal points for proper fit. The goal is to balance a comfortable fit with the performance needs of your style of kayaking. The differences in outfitting for whitewater kayaking, sea and surf kayaking, and recreational kayaking are mostly a matter of degree; the principles are the same. Think of your kayak fit in the same sense you would about your boot and shoe fit. For all sports, your footwear needs to fit well. For climbing you need maximum performance, and a climbing shoe must fit very snugly. When hiking you need a hiking boot to cover the miles with performance and control, but you also need a level of comfort to be able to continue. And with sandals you are maximizing comfort and are outfitted for only minimum control, such as when walking on a beach.

The Seat

Your kayak's seat and the *back band* or *backrest* are the most important components in terms of comfort while paddling. The recumbent position of kayaking is naturally a comfortable one, but your rear end and lower back need to be evenly supported to distribute the weight and avoid pressure points. Make these adjustments in advance, since your options for shifting around and making changes once situated in the kayak and underway are minimal.

In the past seat design by many commercial kayak manufacturers has appeared to have been an afterthought, driven as much by price and ease of installation as by fit. A competitive market has fostered innovations in this area. Nevertheless, it is impossible for any one seat design, even a good one, to fit all possible human shapes. Therefore, your first seat customization decision will be whether to utilize the existing seat as a base and improve its fit or to take it out and

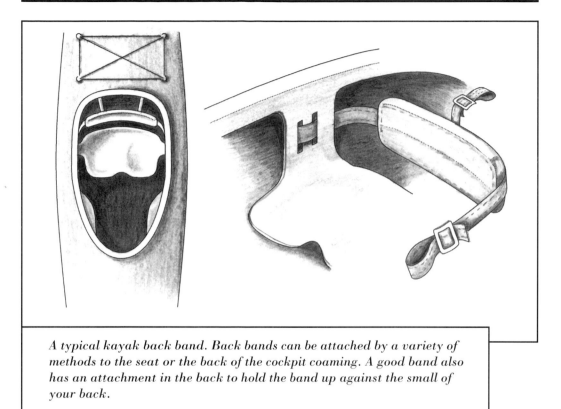

A typical kayak back band. Back bands can be attached by a variety of methods to the seat or the back of the cockpit coaming. A good band also has an attachment in the back to hold the band up against the small of your back.

build from scratch. Either way, a seat designed just for your needs will not be as difficult to create as it may sound.

If you have a new kayak or are new to the sport, put some paddle time in to get a feel for what needs to be done. Before hitting the water, get the *foot pegs* and back support into proper position. Adjust the angle or tension on the back rest/back band to support your lower back and give your back a sense of "gripping" the boat. Adjust the positions of the foot pegs so your knees are bent sufficiently to allow you to grip the thigh braces as well (if so equipped).

With these points adjusted, you should feel sufficiently wedged in to be able to hold yourself in the kayak even if it were upside-down (which is what you would be if trying to execute a roll). If you are uncomfortable with this snug a fit, back off on these settings. You can fine-tune these positions later as you customize your fit and as your paddling confidence grows.

After being on the water, you can identify areas for improvement. Does the contour of the present seat match your anatomy and remain comfortable for extended periods? Make note of any pressure points, including the front edge of the seat where it may pinch a leg nerve and put your leg to sleep. Try a few wet exits and see how easy it is to hold yourself in for a few moments and also how easy it is to relax your legs and slide out. Practice some *leaned turns*, *braces*, and *sweep strokes* to determine if the seat is too wide and how much hip support you may want. If taking a kayak skills course, pay attention to these fit issues and seek opinions from knowledgeable instructors.

A cockpit fit kit from Dagger with preshaped minicell hip and seat pads, contact adhesive, sandpaper, and dragonskin.

Most kayaks come with an installed contoured seat. For extra comfort, fill in with minicell foam some of the contours or add some padding. Generally you don't want to add too much height to the seat: even a small increase in the position of your center of gravity will noticeably decrease the kayak's stability. As you experiment with the fit, lightly tape the foam pieces in place, and then go for a test paddle to see how it works before committing to that configuration with adhesive. Proceed carefully and patiently when modifying the seat's comfort and fit. In the end, you'll have to sit with it.

If all you want for your posterior is a softer, more comfortable surface, there are a number of commercially made seat pads and cushions that will do the job. Many paddlesports accessory suppliers offer basic minicell foam seat pads that fit the contours of most molded hard seats. For a more deluxe ride, you can use gel-filled pads. The gel flows into the correct shape and eliminates pressure points. Planetary Gear makes this variety of pad that is held in place with Velcro and a security cord.

Several inflatable seat cushions are available, including one by Cascade Designs that is patterned after the construction of their popular Therm-a-REST sleeping pads. With it, you can vary the amount of air you sit on, striking a balance of comfort and performance.

Other products are coming onto the market all the time. Look through the ads in paddlesports-specific magazines (see chapter 8) or check your local paddlesports store for more possibilities. If you are looking for new outfitting ideas, go to where the kayaks are. Kayak events like rodeos, races, and symposiums bring paddlers and manufacturers together, and the latest ideas—the good, the bad, and the ugly—will be there as well. When it comes to finding the best seat arrangement, your needs may be relatively unique, so be prepared to look around.

Minicell fitting pad with shaping tool and dragonskin.

WORKING WITH MINICELL FOAM

Minicell has become one of the most useful ingredients for outfitting canoes and kayaks. A dense, but light, closed-cell foam, minicell is easy to cut and shape, resists compression, and tolerates a fair amount of wear and tear. Virtually any effort to customize the fit of a kayak involves the use of some minicell foam. Here are some general points about working with it.

- **Cutting and shaping.** You can get minicell in various preshaped pieces or in bulk sheets from a number of vendors. The foam is relatively expensive, so plan ahead, cut carefully, and save any significant pieces. It can be cut with a variety of sharp tools, including a hacksaw blade or an old bread knife. For more precise shaping and smoothing, use a metal sandpaper commonly called dragonskin or a shaping tool such as a Stanley Sureform.

- **Adhesives.** Paddlesports stores commonly sell quality contact adhesives like Hydrogrip and Mondo Bond. Follow directions carefully; these adhesives generally require coating both surfaces and setting until tacky before joining.

- **Safety.** When working with minicell foam or any other material that will change the way you fit in your kayak, keep the entrapment issue in mind. In the worst-case scenario, you must instinctively be able to release your legs and slide out of the cockpit. Practice wet exits with a new customizing job in safe water before venturing out onto more technical water. The snugness of your kayak fit should grow with your increasing skills of braces and a solid roll in the conditions in which you paddle.

INSTALLING A NEW SEAT

Replacing an existing seat or installing a new one is a more ambitious project, and you should consider a number of things before removing your existing seat. First, have a clear idea what it is you want to do, what materials and tools the job will require, and how long it will take, because you won't be able to paddle the kayak in the meantime. When removing the old seat, be sure you are not altering any structural parts of the kayak. Particularly with whitewater boats, stock seats may be part of the system that provides rigidity to the hull or holds the pillars in place. If so, you must accommodate these structural features in your new design.

If removing a hanging fiberglass seat that is built into the coaming, you may want to leave in place a length of the sidewall for use as an anchor point, perhaps for a back band, the new seat, or a set of hip pads. Keep the original "sitting" part of the seat for mounting at a different angle or height or as a template for another seat.

An important issue to consider is the effect of the position of the seat on the *balance point* of the kayak. In some cases, this may be the primary reason for modifying or repositioning a seat. Since your body weight is such a high percentage of the weight of the kayak when in the water, even small changes in the seat position can have noticeable effects on the way the boat handles. These changes in the trim—or the waterline shape of the kayak—will determine how the hull turns, how it reacts when crossing an eddyline, and how it is influenced by the wind (*weather-cocking*), among other effects. So unless you are certain of what you are doing, try not to move this balance point. Use a measurable reference, such as the line defined by your hipbones, as a way to note where the seat should be positioned.

Some kayaks may have some adjustability built into the design of the seat to allow for fine-tuning the trim. You can also control the trim by how you load the kayak. The farther from the center that a given item is stored, the more its weight will affect the trim. Too much heavy stuff toward the ends of the kayak will increase the *swing weight* and make for sluggish turning.

As mentioned earlier, maintain a low center of gravity for the boat. Unless you need clearance above the cockpit coaming—say for a paddler with a short torso—keep the thickness of a new seat arrangement to a minimum. When removing an old seat, make a few measurements of its height above the *keel line* of the hull for future reference.

If you find a commercially made seat that fills your needs and is available as a separate accessory, you need to determine if its width, shape, and method of attachment is compatible with your kayak's cockpit. Most likely some sort of dissimilarity will require drilling, gluing, or shimming with foam.

Creating a new seat from raw materials is not as difficult as it may sound. The easiest base material to work with is likely to be minicell foam. Making a simple platform for some of the commercially-available cushions or padded seats is probably the simplest route and will provide adequate comfort for many paddlers. The trickiest part of the operation is shaping the underside of the piece of foam to match the contour of the hull at the point where you want to install it.

First, make a template of the contour of the hull. Do this by measuring along a given line and transferring those numbers to a piece of cardboard, which will be your template cutout. Use the line defined by the front edge of the foam seat platform. The rear edge of the seat platform is likely to have essentially the same contour unless your kayak has a pronounced taper or *V-hull*. Another way to create a template is to bend a piece of pliable metal like a coat hanger into the correct shape. (Another useful item for this purpose is the aluminum stay out of an internal-frame backpack). Use the template to check the contour of the underside of the seat foam as you cut it to shape.

A complete seat can be fashioned from minicell foam. Ken Rasmussen's article in *Sea Kayaker* on seat construction (see chapter 8) has become one of the definitive works detailing a method for doing this. In addition to useful methods for making a positioning template and shaping the foam to the contour of your anatomy, Rasmussen makes several good suggestions, including the use of a custom seat to lower the center of gravity and tips on covering the shaped foam with a fabric for added durability.

Hip Pads

Hip pads can be built into your custom arrangement to prevent slipping sideways while executing leaned turns and bracing strokes. If you fit them snugly, hip pads make it easier to stay in position in the kayak without straining against the foot pedals or tensing your legs. Curving the pads outward at the tops produces even more of a grip on your hips. Keep in mind, however, the importance of both a tight fit and a quick exit from the cockpit in an emergency.

A variety of commercially-made kits—minicell being the material of choice—are available. Such whitewater kayak companies as Perception, Dagger, Wave Sport, and Prijon supply hip pad fit kits with their boats. Some newer kayak models have width-adjustable seats that eliminate all or most of the cutting and gluing. Also, several accessory companies, including Planetary Gear and North Shore, Inc., also distribute hip pads and other outfitting pads. Some of these sets are pretty basic—just shaped minicell pads that are glued into place. More deluxe models have foam sections encased in nylon, allowing for different widths, with Velcro or strap attachment methods that eliminate the need to use adhesive. These deluxe alternatives give more adjustability between different kayaks or between different users.

Making your own hip pads is quite simple. Cut the foam into the approximate shapes and depth you want—usually about 4 by 4 inches (10 by 10 cm) or 4 by 6 inches (10 by 15 cm) will do, depending on the size of the surface to be attached to. When fitting, be sure to allow for the thickness of your paddle clothes. Put the pads in place temporarily with tape and try them out. Once you are satisfied with the fit, then fix them permanently in place with contact adhesive. Use dragonskin to fine-tune the fit as needed.

Back Bands and Backrests

Lower back supports are another aspect of kayak accessory design that has seen a lot of innovation in the last few years. With improvements in padding and the quality of back bands, the trend has been away from rigid or tilting back rests, primarily to provide a greater range of back motion during active kayaking and certain styles of rolls. Your upgrade from one band to another will be smooth if you pick a model with a mounting method compatible with your kayak's construction.

If you're installing your kayak's first back band, you need to determine what on the kayak the back band is attached to. On molded seats that come installed in most polyethylene whitewater and touring kayaks, look for slots for that purpose on the sides. There may be bolts holding the seat in place near the sides of the coaming on the hull; these points are commonly used for back band attachments. You may need to drill holes or slots in the sides of a fiberglass seat. You can avoid dismantling or cutting by creating an attachment point with a length of nylon cord threaded around the seat support and tied off in a loop. Some of the commercially made back bands come with mounting kits that have suggestions specific to that design.

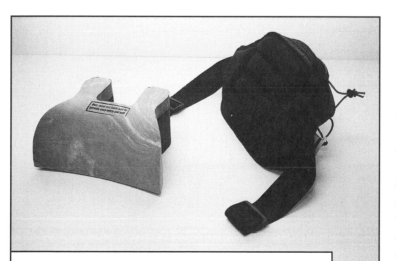

Some lower back support alternatives: a shaped minicell foam support for whitewater kayaks and an adjustable nylon back band with zippered compartment from Planetary Gear.

Usually some sort of support strap or stretch cord is required to hold the band in place so that it meets the small of your back. These support straps attach to the rear pillar, bulkhead, or back edge of the coaming and may interfere slightly with access to the space right behind the seat if you use it for storing gear. On the other hand, the straps can be utilized to help hold things securely in the boat. Several of the more deluxe back band models have zippered pockets that provide storage for an assortment of small items.

Rigid fiberglass and plastic seat backs, though less common now on touring and sea kayaks, are still used on a variety of primarily North American–designed kayaks. They provide lots of back support and often come with an easily adjustable line that controls the amount of tilt. However, rigid seat backs interfere with lower back motion and get in the way of snug-fitting spray skirt designs.

You can trim a bit across the top of some fiberglass seat backs to reduce some of this height. Sand the resulting cut smooth and if necessary touch it up with a bit of epoxy to prevent fraying. A back pad of minicell foam can easily be shaped and glued along the top several inches of the seat back to focus more of the support into the lower lumbar area of the back. If you wish, the rigid seat backs can also be completely removed and replaced with a nylon back band.

Thigh Braces

An effective thigh brace arrangement is the key to holding yourself securely in the kayak and staying in control in complex water conditions. If the surface of the thigh brace wraps around the lower thigh or knee sufficiently, you can grip and hold yourself in the kayak with your legs, allowing more flexibility with your lower back for aggressive paddling maneuvers. Casual paddlers find that a well-fitted set of thigh braces improves leaning and turning techniques, leading to an improvement in most other skills.

Thigh braces supplied with most state-of-the-art whitewater kayaks have improved greatly

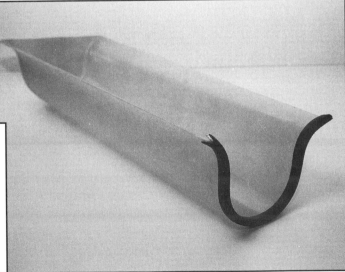

A knee tube is a rigid storage container mounted to the inside foredeck. It can be incorporated into the knee and thigh padding used to provide maximum control of a sea kayak.

over the last few years, and a bit of tinkering with extra minicell foam may be all that is needed for an exact fit. Some kayak models now have sized or adjustable thigh brace options that allow you to fine-tune the fit.

General river touring and casual recreational kayaks are the least likely to have a well-thought-out thigh brace configuration, if any at all. Check with the manufacturer or your paddlesports dealer to see which models have a thigh brace set available as an add-on accessory. Otherwise, it's again time to play around with the minicell foam. A good knee or thigh brace can take on a number of shapes, depending on the inside space and shape of the hull and the amount of support you are seeking. One option for experimenting with possible foam configurations is to use some duct tape and some throwaway Styrofoam, such as a chunk left over from appliance or electronics packaging. Use this to shape some potential thigh brace sets and test them in the kayak. Once satisfied with your creation, you can copy the shape into more durable minicell and install it into the kayak for fine-tuning.

For sea kayaks some of these same options apply. Stock thigh brace systems vary from very good to none at all. Molded thigh braces may be available from some makers of older model kayaks, or there may be some that can be adapted to your kayak. You can retrofit certain composite sea kayaks with a *knee tube*. This fiberglass trough accessory is mounted to the inside of the deck and can be used for storage and as part of a knee-bracing system. It is available from Great River Outfitters, one of the importers of British sea kayaking equipment.

Foot Braces

For many paddlers, the adjustable foot pegs that come installed in most kayaks do the job quite adequately. Their adjustability is an advantage for kayaks used by more than one person or perhaps for conditions requiring different thicknesses of footwear. In situations in which you want to push on a more solid platform or to eliminate the chance of foot entrapment, a foam or bulkhead foot brace may be the way to go. These permanent foot braces are more common in whitewater kayaks because of an increase in techniques that put substantial pressure on these supports. Several whitewater suppliers have bulkhead footbrace kits available, but check for compatibility between models.

You can custom order some models of performance sea kayaks with the glassed-in bulkhead in the correct position for use as a foot brace or in conjunction with a foot-operated pump. This eliminates the need for an installed sliding brace but limits the fit to individuals with a certain leg length. This option, therefore, may not be practical unless you intend to keep the boat for your own use. An added advantage is that by bringing the bulkhead aft a bit, the size of the airtight front compartment is increased, and the floodable cockpit space is reduced.

While tinkering with the foot brace, you may want to put in some small foam pads to cushion or insulate your heels if that is a comfort issue for you.

Again, when experimenting with fitting components, keep in mind the entrapment issue and be certain you can instinctively release from the system and wet exit if necessary. Additionally, for longer distance touring, consider legroom and overall comfort issues. A certain amount of wiggle and stretch space may feel pretty good at times to keep your circulation flowing and allow you to keep focused on the paddling experience.

Sit-on-Top Outfitting

You can incorporate different levels of outfitting to SOTs. A basic sitting position and footrests are usually molded into the hulls of these craft. For longer touring or for maximum comfort, some sort of nylon backrest is the first level of outfitting necessity. These generally have a strap or clip system that allows adjusting the tilt of the backrest. SOTs used for recreational paddling in calm water conditions should not require much more.

A setup for holding the paddler in place is required for sit-on-top kayaks designed for more serious paddling conditions, such as surfing. Without a deck, a SOT requires a thigh strap system similar in principle to those commonly used in whitewater canoes. Several accessory companies, including Mark Pack Works, have components available for this type of outfitting.

Deck Layout

Attachments to the outside deck of a kayak range from nothing in the case of performance slalom kayaks to the overflow storage capacity of an expedition sea kayak. Depending on the type of kayaking, the layout of deck accessories can include a range of personal preferences that are ideal for customizing. Whitewater, racing, and surf kayaks require only the minimum of accessorizing so as to preserve the sleek *hydrodynamic* characteristics of the craft.

There is considerable debate over the subject of how best to accessorize the deck of a touring or sea kayak. With no absolute right or wrong ways to do things, you can choose from good ideas and not-so-good ideas, depending on your style of paddling. Many factors can go into a decision as to where to place an attachment point or carry an accessory. Some paddlers prefer to keep a clean, spartan look to their kayak deck, whether for aesthetic reasons or for the sake of gear security in rough conditions. Others want certain pieces of equipment easily reachable without removing the spray skirt or opening a hatch.

The best approach for most kayakers is to proceed with caution and avoid getting wrapped up with the over accessorized "look" of a fully outfitted expedition sea kayak. One of the joys of the sport, I would be the first to admit, is tinkering around with all the gadgets and their placement. But you will have plenty of time to ponder some of these issues as you put time in on the water and think things out before drilling.

Whitewater Kayaks

Whitewater and slalom kayaks, with their need for sleek, hydrodynamic shapes, both on and under the water, require a minimum of deck attachments for best performance. Almost all models have grab loops or handles, however, for convenience and for rescue considerations, and these have evolved in the last few years into low-profile placements unlikely to get caught in tight spaces between rocks.

Several retrofittable parts can be helpful in certain applications. Drain plugs are useful in kayaks with upturned ends or tightly fitted flotation that inhibit draining all the trapped water out through the cockpit. Simply stand the kayak on end and let gravity do its work. Available from a number of the whitewater kayak manufacturers, drain plug kits are not difficult to install, al-

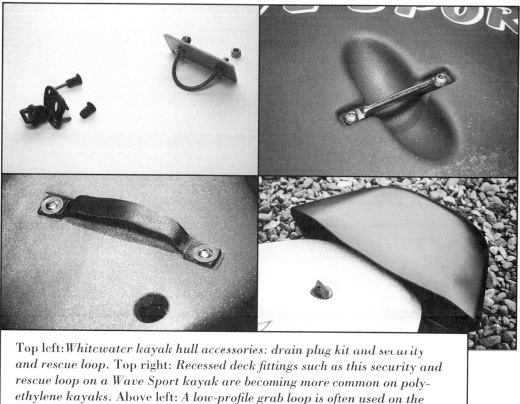

Top left:*Whitewater kayak hull accessories: drain plug kit and security and rescue loop.* Top right: *Recessed deck fittings such as this security and rescue loop on a Wave Sport kayak are becoming more common on poly- ethylene kayaks.* Above left: *A low-profile grab loop is often used on the latest whitewater kayak designs.* Above right: *End caps can be installed on the bow and stern of whitewater kayaks to reduce damage from impacts.*

though they may require a bit of acrobatic dexterity to reach the necessary mounting position from inside the hull. Bow and stern end caps are available for many kayak models. These molded plastic covers reduce some of the damage done to kayaks used in shallow and rocky rivers. They may be rather clunky looking and add weight to the boat but will definitely help prolong the life of the boat for those who tend to trash their kayaks rather quickly.

Sea Kayak Deck Layout

There are as many variations on ways to organize the deck accessories on a sea kayak as there are models of kayaks. The broad categories of British style vs. North American deck layout configurations are very general ones, and the distinctions have become blurred over the past few years.

You will undoubtedly want to modify the following suggestions to your own particular situation. Remember to proceed with caution; you don't have to do everything at once.

If you are in the process of purchasing a special-order kayak and feel strongly about some deck configuration issue, most manufacturers should be willing to install various fittings, such as deck lines and bulkheads, to your specifications or at least provide one without these fittings for your own do-it-yourself job.

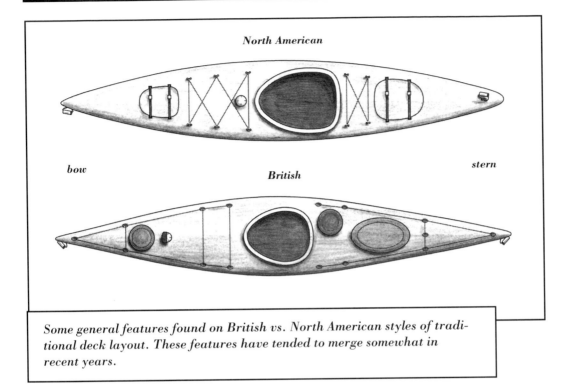

North American

bow   *British*   *stern*

Some general features found on British vs. North American styles of traditional deck layout. These features have tended to merge somewhat in recent years.

PLACING DECK FITTINGS

Plan ahead before you drill holes in your kayak. That sounds obvious, but whereas it is quite simple to install new deck fittings, it is a much greater chore to fill in old or improperly placed holes. The woodworker's adage of "measure twice, cut once" applies to kayak customization as well. Follow these steps for making deck fittings.

1. Choose the fittings you need for your project. Browse around a paddlesports shop or shop for ideas at a kayak symposium.

2. Choose the locations for these fittings on the deck. You may want to do a practice trip with the fittings temporarily duct-taped in place to see if the idea works for you. That area of the deck may need reinforcing in some cases to spread the load out from the fitting.

3. Drill bolt holes to match the bolt diameter. A snug fit may mean no leaks and no further need to caulk or seal.

4. Mount, seal, or trim off the extra bolt length, and don't overtighten the nuts. Self-locking nuts prevent loosening and leaking in the future.

5. Thread the stretch cords or grab lines, if that's what you're doing. Fasten down the ends of stretch cording with electrical tape or nylon *zips*, the one-way fastening loops used to hold bunches of wires together, to prevent untying. Seal or melt the ends of the cords to prevent unraveling.

Deck hardware used
on touring kayaks: pad
eye-type deck fitting.

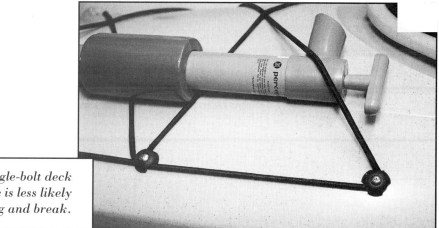

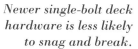

*Newer single-bolt deck
hardware is less likely
to snag and break.*

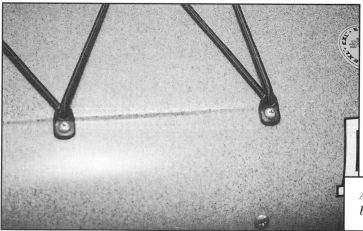

*Another style of single-
bolt deck fitting.*

If you think you may eventually upgrade to another kayak and sell the current model, keep the resale value in mind before adding any exotic or unusually placed fittings.

DECK ACCESSORY STRETCH CORDS

Almost all touring and sea kayaks come with a pattern of stretch cords mounted to the deck just forward of the cockpit. Whether a basic square or a more elaborate figure-8, this configuration of stretch cords is designed to hold down and keep accessible a number of important accessories that are needed throughout the paddling day. First and foremost of these items is a map or chart case, but other commonly carried items typically end up there, including a handheld bilge pump, sunglass case, waterproof pouch for a radio, camera, or GPS unit, flashlight, and so on.

Remember that stretch cords are not a totally secure way to hold things in the event of rough conditions. Be vigilant of the gear on the deck and consider other storage options, including deck bags and pockets in your jacket, PFD, or spray skirt. Secure indispensable items with a clip or short tether or stow them inside the kayak if the going gets rough.

When on long tours, you will be spending lots of time looking at the foredeck and perhaps pondering better ways of arranging deck accessories. Changing the position of existing deck fittings requires filling holes, but adding new fittings for special purposes is not difficult. A deck bag or compass mount accessories may require specially located fittings. Look at different brands of kayaks when possible and swap ideas with fellow paddlers for imaginative layouts of deck cords. Take a cautious approach to these projects, however, and do a trial trip with the duct tape method to test out a proposed layout.

As for other deck-mounted accessories, some paddlers prefer to carry a spare paddle on the foredeck, as it is more readily accessible without reaching behind. Especially suited to this deck location is the *Greenland storm paddle*, which is short enough to fit in one piece on most bows. One disadvantage of having paddles and other items too far forward is the splash factor—in choppy conditions, waves washing over the fore deck can hit this gear and cause splashes that inevitably seem to splatter your face.

STERN DECK RIGGING

A rectangular pattern of stretch cord on the deck immediately behind the cockpit, which can be utilized as part of the paddle float self-rescue technique, is now often standard equpment. Paddle-float rescues can be done successfully without relying on these placements, but this rigging may be useful for practice or for setting up the paddle and float as an *outrigger* for some other purpose, such as photography. I am leery of the stress that a rigging-anchored paddle and float put on the blade or shaft of the paddle in choppy or breaking waves. These stretch cords can be useful for stowing certain pieces of gear, such as a partially inflated *paddle float* or a hydration system. If customizing a deck without this setup, you may find alternate uses for this space.

Another common use of stern deck space is for carrying a spare take-apart paddle, which needs to be accessible in a hurry in some kinds of mishaps. Two short lines of stretch cord can be rigged up to snugly hold down the paddle in such a way to make it reasonably easy to slide out when needed. The exact position of the paddle will depend on the shape of the deck, and in most cases it will have to straddle the rear hatch.

SAFETY GRAB LINES

Bow and stern safety grab lines, a feature found on British-made kayaks for many years, are increasingly becoming standard on North American kayaks. These lines enable a paddler in the water to have something to hold onto while maneuvering into position for a rescue or for quickly retrieving the kayak after a capsize. For this application, stretch cord material has too much play, so a static cord, usually polypropylene, is used. These lines are generally installed through recessed deck fittings, which reduce the chance of clothing or gear getting hung up while doing rescues involving the deck.

You may want to add your own safety lines if your kayak doesn't have them. Unless you want to undertake some intricate fiberglass work, recessed fittings are not practical, but some of the newer snag-resistant fittings are the next best alternative. Because of the possibility of a heavy force being placed on them, mount the fittings in a structurally stiff part of the deck near an edge or the curve leading into the seam. On lighter decks that can be flexed with the push of a thumb, place a reinforcing patch on the inside surface to give additional support. Safety lines should extend far enough toward the bow and stern grab loops so that one line or another is within reach by a person in the water.

GRAB HANDLES

Virtually all kayaks have some variation of bow and stern handles or loops built into them. These serve various purposes in addition to being a means of carrying the kayak around. Like deck safety lines, grab handles can provide an important point to hold onto and are essential in windy conditions and surf. The *toggle*, or handle part of the loop, should allow a firm handgrip on the outside of the cord, so that if the kayak twists around, fingers won't get trapped in the loop. A good toggle will also be more comfortable when carrying a loaded boat for any distance.

The grab handles are often used as tie-down points for car-topping, which probably produces the most wear and tear of any of their uses. Maintain the integrity of the cord in the loops for this purpose, as well as for towing in a rescue. You can upgrade the handle configuration when it comes time to replace this cord, or sooner if need be.

The cord should enter and exit the toggle relatively close together to prevent pinched fingers. Use a durable nylon, nylon-sheathed polypropylene cord, or Spectra cord for abrasion resistance in a diameter that allows the knot to be tied and worked inside the toggle. Replacement toggles are available from a number of manufacturers, or if you prefer you can make one yourself using a small section of PVC piping. Cut, drill and sand the pipe into service. The grab handles of some older kayaks and basic

A grab handle kit with U-bolt mount. This would require reaching deep into the hull of the kayak to install.

recreational kayaks may simply be loops of cord bonded into the hull. When replacing these, it may be simplest to cut them off and start from scratch.

If relocating or installing a kayak's first grab handles, each should be as close to the tip of the kayak as possible, although in the stern a rudder may interfere with this location. If the kayak has an *end pour*—a filler material bonded into the last six inches or so of the bow and stern— then a hole can be drilled through the hull at the desired point to accommodate the cord. If need be, doing an end pour can be a major project that involves propping the kayak on end and rigging a method of getting the filler into the end space without making a mess. Some of the building-related books listed in chapter 8's bibliography describe this process in detail.

I have seen several recent kayak models with grab handles that are held neatly on the deck with a Velcro tab. They are a nice touch if you don't like the grab handles flopping around, but make sure they are accessible for safety purposes.

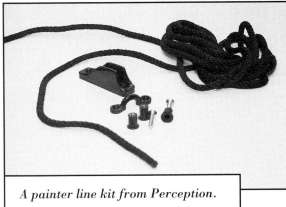

A painter line kit from Perception.

PAINTER LINES

Painter lines are another useful deck accessory preferred by some paddlers, myself included. These lines are attached to the bow and can be used for a number of purposes, including tying off to a dock or other landing point when you want to leave the kayak in the water, securing the kayak on a beach where waves or tides could pull it off, or *lining* the kayak through a shallow area or up a stream. You can thread the painter through the grab handle hole, if there is enough space, and tie it off with a figure-8 knot or tie it directly to the grab handle cord.

Depending on your specific needs, about 10 to 15 feet (3 to 4.6 m) should be a sufficient length. Cinch off the free end of the line at a *jam cleat* or run to a *T-cleat* and back to the bow loop. I have tied a small brass clip to the end of my painter for convenience in attaching the line to things. If you desire, a stern painter can also be utilized as part of the system.

PADDLE LEASHES

A *paddle leash* can be used in various configurations, some of which can generate a considerable debate over the pros and cons of such use. In its simplest form, a short line or section of stretch cord can be used as a *paddle park*. While the paddler rests or does something else, the paddle can be allowed to float next to the kayak out of the way. A substantial strip of Velcro is the easiest way to attach the line to the paddle shaft. This technique avoids the need to tie a knot or take the paddle apart to slip on a loop. An alternative method uses a wrist loop with a small ball on the end that the paddler wears with the other end attached to the paddle. The ball end can be slipped under a deck line to park the paddle.

A paddler-to-paddle leash helps hold onto the paddle in the event of a capsize, but the risk of getting tangled or clobbered if you let go of the paddle is always there. A paddle leash connec-

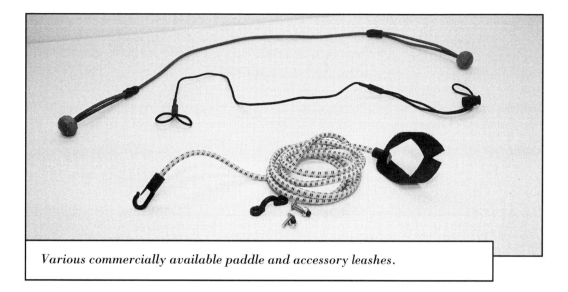

Various commercially available paddle and accessory leashes.

tion from the kayak deck to the paddle is used with the idea that, in a capsize and a missed roll, you retain control over the kayak as long as you hold onto the paddle. Again the danger is one of entanglement in a line if things go wrong. This danger must be weighed against the possibility in open water of having the kayak blow away faster than you can swim. Either possibility is serious, but the underlying issue is one of skills practice so that it is not likely to happen in the first place. It is a bit like the mountaineering debate over the use of a safety leash on an ice axe; whether falling with a flailing axe attached to your arm is worse than losing it altogether is an unpleasant choice that proper practice can largely avoid.

I have heard of paddlers that use a tether running from the paddler to the kayak, but without some sort of foolproof quick-release system, this would involve an even greater chance of entanglement. This could be particularly true in high winds or surf where the kayak might rotate around and around, not something I would want my foot or arm attached to.

HATCH COVERS

Some of the many varieties of hatch designs on modern sea kayaks come with tethers connected to the hatch covers for added security. If you are the sort of paddler who likes as many backup systems as possible, installing a hatch tether or attaching some foam flotation to them is not a difficult project. Though rare, you could lose a cover in a number of ways. Although opening a hatch while underway on the open water is generally poor practice, the necessity may arise. A hatch cover could be dropped while loading or unloading a kayak from the awkward position on a dock or wharf. And of course there is always the possibility of merrily driving off into the sunset on the interstate with the hatches unfastened.

Fiberglass hatch covers in particular will not float. The round VCP (Valley Canoe brand) or similar hatches found on many kayaks will float slightly but being black may not be very visible in the water. For a retaining tether, you need enough cord—⅛-inch nylon should do—to reach from an attachment point inside the compartment to the hatch cover when it is placed out of the way while loading. You can anchor the inside attachment point to some existing bolt, a mirrored fitting as described later, or a small *D-ring* bonded into place. On the cover, an attachment point can be affixed with structural adhesive or epoxy. Tether polyethylene hatch covers that utilize an interior neoprene cover to the outside of the kayak. As for rubber hatch covers, you can use a small stainless bolt, mounted into the top surface and reinforced with wide diameter washers, as a tether point.

An alternative to tethering is making the hatch light enough to float. Do this by bonding enough minicell foam to the underside of the cover to give it buoyancy. It won't take as much foam as you might think, so experiment before the final bonding job. The foam will take up an inch or so of space under the hatch cover, but should not be enough to affect the amount of packing space.

COMPASS MOUNTS

One of the key pieces of navigational equipment for serious touring is the deck-mounted *reciprocal compass*. Most of the top-of-the-line sea kayaks now have some sort of spot molded onto the deck for the purpose of attaching a compass. Exactly how and where this is done may warrant being a consideration when you purchase a particular kayak model.

On some British-designed kayaks, recessed compass mounts are positioned well forward of the central deck area. This recessed area is limited to specific compass models, usually a top-quality Silva or Suunto marine model. The forward position reduces the angle that a paddler's eyes need to drop from the horizon to read the dial; you need good eyesight for reading at this distance, however. By recessing the compass housing, it becomes protected from possible damage during over-the-bow rescues and from errant paddle strokes.

A flat compass-mount area at the peak of the foredeck accommodates a greater variety of compass models, but exposes the compass to more hits from equipment or scratches if and when the kayak is turned upside-down. Several popular compass models, including Perception's Aquameter, have a snap-off base allowing the compass to be removed when desired. A compass mounted within 12 inches (30 cm) or so of the front of the cockpit may interfere with the prime space for a map case spread out under the stretch cords.

Clip-on compass mounts create a small flat platform suitable for mounting a compass on kayaks that have no flat place to attach a compass to. Available from a number of kayak accessory distributors, the compass clips are usually connected by stretch cords, which are attached to the

A clip-on deck compass mount from Perception.

deck lines. These compasses are easily removable—perhaps too much so, if you are inclined to paddle in the rough stuff. However, one advantage of this setup is moving the compass easily from one kayak to another if you have more than one.

A few compass models have optional lights available for night paddling. Check carefully to see what type of battery power they require and what it will take to keep the batteries waterproof. A less expensive option for the occasional night paddle is to use a chemical light stick, Cyalume or other imitations, taped to the deck in such a way as to illuminate the dial. The color red is easiest on your night vision, by the way. You can rig up a short piece of stretch cord on the deck to act as a light stick holder for these rare occasions.

RUDDERS AND SKEGS

The pros and cons of rudders and skegs have been discussed previously, and you will have to evaluate their value to you based on your paddling style and needs. Upgrading and adding rudders, and to a lesser extent, skegs, is a relatively common procedure, particularly on polyethylene kayaks that are often sold in "basic" or "standard" versions without some of the extras that usually come with the "expedition" models or with composite-hull kayaks. Most manufacturers of kayaks with rudders will offer some kind of rudder upgrade kit to match their boats, and some of these kits may work on other models and brands as well. Expect to pay around $200 for these kits, if they include the necessary foot pedals. One of the most reliable is the Feathercraft rudder, which is used on many different makes of kayaks.

Before investing the time and money, consider what it is you are trying to accomplish with the upgrade. A rudder or skeg is primarily a tracking aid in certain types of crosswinds and following seas, particularly useful for saving some energy on longer cruises. If your kayak seems completely unmanageable in these and other conditions, or your kayak-handling skills haven't progressed to where you can yet evaluate the difference, then the rudder system may only be a crutch on a boat that may no longer suit your needs. If possible, try out some other styles and models of touring kayaks and take some instructional courses to be better able to decide on the best plan of action.

With that said, let's look at some of the elements that make for a good rudder system and what it takes to fit it on an existing kayak. Rudder design has come a long way in the last ten or fifteen years, so don't necessarily stick with components that work but go back a long way. The most important feature to look for is the ability of the rudder blade to flip up out of the way onto the rear deck when not in use. This keeps the blade out of harm's way when approaching the shore or other hazards and also allows the blade to pivot and ride over obstructions in the water. The flip-up feature takes one or two lines, depending on the brand, to raise and lower the blade, and these should operate smoothly and quickly with one hand. The blade should be relatively long and narrow, so that it stays in the water if choppy waves lift the stern out of the water.

How maintenance-friendly will the system be once installed—are bolts and other parts accessible and workable with reasonably common tools? How the rudder housing attaches to the stern of the kayak is critical; a handcrafted or unusual kayak design may require some serious modifications. If a particular rudder requires a *pivot pin or axle* mounted into the stern, an end pour of filler may need to be made, and the existing stern grab handle will most likely have to be moved.

The cables connecting the rudder housing with the foot pedals have to enter the kayak hull at some point; exactly where will depend on the contours of the deck, the location of other deck

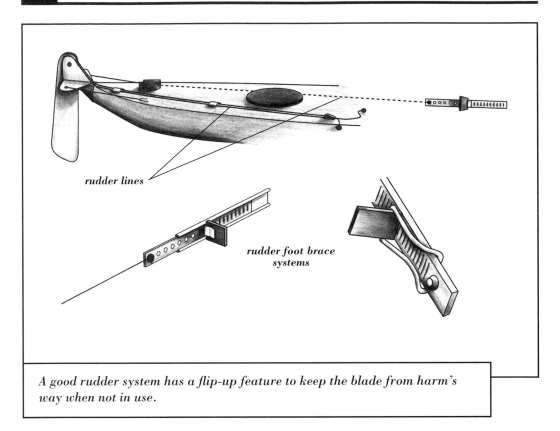

rudder lines

rudder foot brace systems

A good rudder system has a flip-up feature to keep the blade from harm's way when not in use.

accessories, and so on. Fewer bends or curves in the cable path produce a smoother operation. Following the advice of the particular kit is a good starting point, but you may have preferences as to whether you want the cables exposed on the rear deck or running along the hull inside the boat. If you don't want to compromise the integrity of the stern compartment by having the cables run through it, pass the cable through a channel of plastic tubing. This will protect the cable and any gear packed near it.

To control the rudder blade's range of motion, most rudder systems use sliding foot pedals connected to the cables. To accommodate different leg lengths, the cable length or the cable attachment point to the pedal must be adjustable.

A classic problem of rudder systems is that the sliding pedals used to control the rudder reduce the ability of the paddler to stay braced in position and effectively control the kayak. Some rudder systems have a slot or wedge built into the rear deck to hold the upright rudder blade in a locked position, thus preventing the cables and the foot pedals from moving. There is a certain amount of looseness in this setup, however, and it doesn't solve the problem for situations when one may want to brace, lean, and rudder at the same time, as in a turbulent following sea.

The need for a fixed-position foot peg with a rotating control for the rudder cables was the impetus for one of my early innovations. For many years, I used such a configuration cooked up by a paddling friend in a machine shop. Mounted into a 15-foot (4.6 m) touring kayak, it gave me control over weathercocking with a rudder in breezy conditions while still allowing for strong braces and carved turns. Several kayak manufacturers, including Prijon and Seaward, now have fixed-position foot pegs available on various kayak models. The system developed by Seaward Kayaks allows for easy adjustments in both leg length and pedal angle while giving a firm platform for serious bracing. You can purchase this pedal system separately for retrofitting other makes of kayaks.

UCO, a manufacturer of candle lanterns and other machined accessories for the camping market, has just released an integrated foot brace-rudder system. This system also offers fixed-position foot pedals that may be incorporated into several kayak lines and is expected to be available as a retrofittable option, as well. Details are still sketchy, but my hunch is that this system may become something of a milestone in accessory design.

The possibilities for retrofitting a skeg onto an existing kayak are more limited. The best retractable skeg configurations involve an enclosed housing built into the hull in the stern compartment, an ambitious fiberglassing project for most do-it-yourselfers and virtually impossible in polyethylene hulls. A basic drop-down skeg arrangement is used by Dagger and others, which is mounted on the stern in a

A fixed-position rudder control pedal used by the author in the early 1980s.

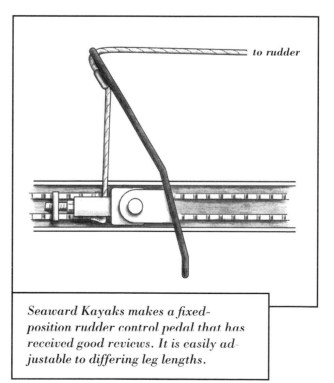

to rudder

Seaward Kayaks makes a fixed-position rudder control pedal that has received good reviews. It is easily adjustable to differing leg lengths.

similar fashion as a rudder without the pivoting capabilities, eliminating the need for cables and modified foot braces. A single line raises and lowers the blade in increments and helps the skeg blade control weathercocking in crosswinds.

Recreational Kayaks

For nontechnical river touring and lake touring kayaks, many sea kayaking deck layout ideas can be put to good use. The two indispensable ones in my opinion, if you are into any kind of exploration, are the use of a compass and a map fastened to the deck for ease of referral. The raised-profile, *reciprocal* compasses commonly used for serious sea kayaking are easy to read and use, but even a basic base-plate hiking compass is handy if you want to avoid the $40 to $100 cost of the others. Having a map or chart visible in a waterproof map case on the deck is also convenient, allowing you to keep track of your position without periodically rummaging in the cockpit for the map.

A simple four-point pattern of stretch cord installed on the deck in front of the coaming will hold down a map case, a clip-on compass mount, and perhaps a few other small items. There are no hard and fast rules on exactly where to place the deck hardware. Just make sure there is enough clearance in front of the tip of the coaming to provide an unrestricted grip on the grab loop of the spray skirt and that there is enough clearance on the sides so that items being held down do not interfere with the forward paddle stroke.

Other sea kayak deck layout ideas may or may not be as useful on basic touring kayaks. In most situations, keeping your gear stowed inside keeps the weight low, reduces the chances of loss, and lessens the surface area presented to the wind. Skegs and rudders can be useful on shorter kayaks to control weathercocking in open-water conditions, but if you find yourself doing a lot of that type of paddling, you may want to consider getting a longer, more seaworthy kayak.

Interior Customizing

Besides the seat, a number of other useful tweaks and modifications can be made to the inside of your kayak to fine-tune its performance and keep miscellaneous gear organized. Remember that any projects undertaken should be done with the escape issue in mind.

Whitewater Kayaks

As whitewater playboats get shorter and lower in volume to facilitate control over the boat, the amount of free space for storing necessities has become limited. Manufacturers are compensating for the lack of storage space, building in placements for items such as water bottles by molding out fitted slots in the seat structure or support pillar. Back bands may have small pockets to hold keys, snacks, and other necessities.

Recreational Kayaks and Sea Kayaks

Several interior customizing ideas are applicable in varying degrees to either touring kayaks or open-water sea kayaks. How useful some of these ideas are will depend on how much gear you are usually carrying around and how much you just like to tinker around.

INTERIOR TIE-DOWN POINTS

Interior tie-down and attachment points for gear can be useful for almost any kayak. Unless you always paddle with a full load with everything wedged into a stable position, your dry bags, containers, and other loose items can shift, becoming inaccessible or throwing off the weight distribution. In the event of an unintended capsize, gear located in the cockpit area can float away and be lost. A series of tie-down points used with stretch cords or tethers can help secure your gear.

The possible locations and varieties of these attachment points are almost endless. The interior space available in your kayak, the type of gear you most frequently carry, and the nature of the water conditions you will be paddling will enter into the planning of where to put them. Most touring kayaks have a number of small spaces that can be utilized for gear storage. Some kayaks have a lot of space immediately behind the seat, which is ideal for day-use items. Wider kayaks may have enough space for storing water bottles or similar sized things between the side of the seat and the hull. You may even have usable space between the forward bulkhead and the foot pegs.

Once you have a use for a particular space, figure out what it will take to hold in place the items to be stored there. Often a simple tether or loop of stretch cord can be attached to an existing part of the kayak, such as a back band or the side of a molded seat. In some cases, an additional deck fitting can be attached to the bolts that hold down an existing fitting on the outside of the deck. You can then tie or bungee things to these *mirrored fittings*. You may need to replace the existing bolts with longer ones to do this.

If you need an attachment point on the sides or the hull floor, it is not difficult to install D-rings of the type commonly used for outfitting whitewater canoes. Smaller sizes, of an inch or less, will be adequate for these tasks. Avoid corrosion by using stainless steel or durable plastic. The rigid plastic-base D-rings produce a stronger bond to composite hulls than do vinyl-base D-rings. Use a urethane structural adhesive and follow directions for best results.

An additional storage area where tie-down points can be useful is the bulkheaded compartment, where water containers, fuel bottles, and other heavy objects should be firmly held down. Also, the space immediately under the front deck ahead of the cockpit is potentially a space where long, narrow objects such as a hand pump, rolled-up map case, or a mesh bag with a rain jacket can be held in place by an attached shock cord pattern.

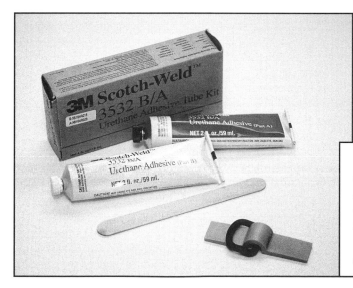

Two-part structural adhesive with plastic D-ring. These D-rings and other fittings can be mounted in the kayak interior as tie-down points for gear and flotation.

BULKHEADS

There may occasionally be situations in which you want to add, reinstall, or move a bulkhead. Adding a bulkhead to a polyethylene touring kayak is probably the most likely scenario. Many of these boats are sold in a basic configuration to keep the price down. These manufacturers usually have bulkheads or a complete installation kit available. If you decide to go this route, you will also have to add hatches to gain access to the bulkhead compartments. Although the compartments will add convenience and needed flotation, this effort should be weighed against the alternative of using flotation-storage bags when you go out on the water.

There may also be good reasons to move the position of an existing kayak bulkhead, but this may require a fair amount of work. One possible reason would be to move one or both bulkheads closer to the center of the kayak to reduce the floodable volume of the cockpit and increase flotation. Bulkheads made of foam are the easiest to remove and replace. Because of the increasing circumference of the kayak toward the center, one or two new bulkheads will have to be created. With luck, the larger of the two old ones can be reshaped and used again. You can make a template out of cardboard, using a series of measurements or a stiff wire to create the shape. Cut and tape as necessary to fine-tune, and then transfer the pattern to the piece of foam and tweak the fit with dragonskin. Lexel polyurethane caulk or a urethane structural adhesive should do the trick of sealing the bulkheads into position.

Newer polyethylene kayaks often have molded plastic bulkheads welded into position, and some composite kayaks have bulkheads made from a fiberglass laminate. Being quite durable, they are probably best left alone. For the average do-it-yourself project, a foam bulkhead is still the best bet. If you are experienced in fiberglass work and willing to work in a confined space, then a glass bulkhead would not be too difficult to make and install.

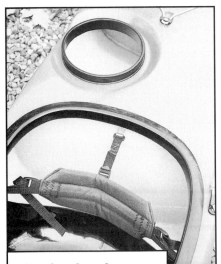

Day hatch and arrangement of stern bulkheads in a NDK Romany sea kayak.

DAY HATCHES

Day hatches are an increasingly popular sea-kayak feature. They essentially create a third bulkheaded compartment located immediately behind the seat and are used for carrying items needed during the course of a normal paddling day. They reduce the need to carry many items on the deck or loose in the cockpit and also help to reduce the amount of volume in the cockpit, thus aiding flotation. You typically get to the space through a round VCP-type hatch cover.

On some models of kayaks, it may be possible to build a day hatch into the existing space behind the seat. The compartment must be long enough, front to back, to accommodate the hatch opening. VCP hatches can be obtained as a complete kit from the importer, Great River Outfitters, or one of their dealers. Smaller, screw-on access portholes are available from marine dealers. If there is much of a contour to the deck at that point, some creative fiberglass or gasket work may be needed to fit the hatch.

PUMPS

Optional bailing pumps can be retrofitted into most sea kayaks. The hand-operated and foot-operated models are designed for the relatively low volume cockpits of British kayaks but will fit into many other models if desired. The foot-operated varieties seem to be gaining in popularity since they free up the hands for paddling and bracing in rough conditions. These foot pumps generally attach to the front bulkhead, so a customized bulkhead position may be necessary for best operation. To help these pumps to get virtually all water out of the boat, an accessory attachment called a *strum box* can be mounted onto the intake hose to create suction in tiny depths of water.

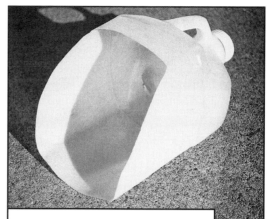

A back-up bailer made from a gallon plastic bottle. A squarish shape is most efficient at getting the last remaining drops. A handheld or installed pump, however, is indispensable during on-the-water rescues.

A small number of paddlers advocate the use of electric bilge pumps, particularly in larger single kayaks and doubles. You can obtain several models and sizes of portable pumps that operate on batteries from marine distributors. These pumps move water as fast or faster than the human-powered models and can be used for a number of cycles on one set of batteries or battery charge. Although the pumps themselves are fairly reliable, any system that utilizes electrical parts in a water environment needs to be tested and used with caution. These pumps have a discharge hose that will need to be exited somewhere on the deck, unless you want to run the hose out manually through the cockpit when needed. The pump will need to be mounted at a low point of the cockpit compartment floor, most likely just behind the seat.

In most situations, it's a good idea to carry a handheld pump, or even the basic cut-off plastic gallon jug, as a backup bailing method. Mechanical pumps are generally quite reliable but still can fail, clog, freeze, or sometimes just be in the wrong position.

Customizing Equipment

You can modify or customize your favorite kayaking accessories in a number of ways to match your paddling needs. Before you begin any project, keep in mind the limitations of the original piece of equipment, and then decide how much energy you want to invest into that item. A heavy paddle with its blades skillfully trimmed down is still going to be a heavy paddle. If what you really want is a higher performance paddle, it may pay in the long run to upgrade to something new and use the time saved for more paddling. The old paddle can become a valuable spare, the old skirt can be used for pool practice, and so on. Nevertheless, most people get great satisfaction using their creative energies to make something do a better job, to extend its useful life, and save a bit of money.

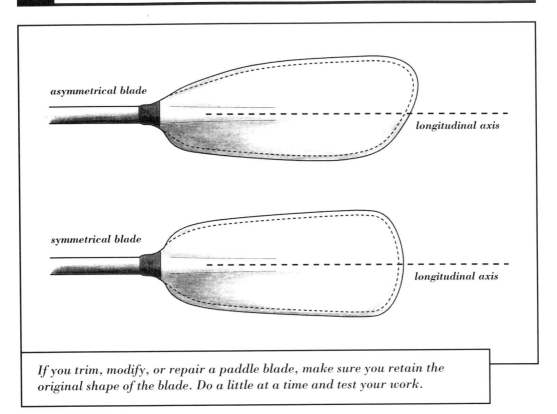

If you trim, modify, or repair a paddle blade, make sure you retain the original shape of the blade. Do a little at a time and test your work.

Paddles

I have seen two noticeable trends over the last few years in both whitewater and touring paddles toward shorter lengths and to slightly smaller blades. Several factors have probably contributed to this trend, including an increased awareness of performance paddling techniques, more women entering the sport, and the greater number of smaller volume "play" or day-tripping kayaks. The result: a lot of longer and bigger paddles are out there that don't get used, and the question of cutting these down to make them smaller then arises.

First, as to the issue of blade size, a smaller blade area allows for a faster *paddling cadence* without increasing the load on the paddle and your arms and shoulders. Most blade materials—wood, composite, or molded plastic—can be trimmed down within limits and with certain exceptions. The proportional shape of the blade, especially the area on each side of the long axis of the blade, should be retained. In other words, don't just trim away on one side.

Proceed with caution: mark your cut lines carefully, use a fine-toothed saw or hacksaw blade, and sand smooth. Exceptions to this procedure include blades with Kevlar, which is very difficult to cut and sand; blades with some sort of built-in edge reinforcement; and some foam-injected blades, in which the outer surface is harder and denser than the core. If you have doubts about any of these parameters, make a small test cut that can be filled with epoxy if you decide to retreat or contact the paddle manufacturer for alternate advice.

Trying to shorten a paddle will create more problems. Merely cutting length out of the blades is not an answer—it is the paddle's shaft length that determines its functional length. Some shafts, particularly composite, may have selective reinforcing around the take-apart joint or the ends that should not be cut away. On some models of paddles, the blades have flanges that are inserted into the shaft. Depending on the adhesive used, it may be possible to get one of these blades off and shorten the shaft. Again, check with the paddle manufacturer for advice on your particular situation. Many of these companies are relatively small and are able to offer various repair services or work with their dealers' and customers' special needs. Keep in mind that major modifications to a paddle or other product is likely to void any warranty that may be in effect.

The popular *ovaled shaft* feature gives an instant feel as to the alignment of the blade. Some manufacturers achieve this by adding a shaped extension to the shaft, usually in the section gripped by the right hand (on an *asymmetrical-blade paddle*). This type of grip can be created on a round shaft by taping a shaped triangular length of minicell foam, about a third of an inch thick, in the grip area on the side of the shaft away from the *power face* of the blade. Use a wide electrical or heat-shrink tape for a smooth surface.

Another paddle enhancement that is easy to install is a set of *drip rings*. Primarily used for kayak touring, where there is a chance of keeping your hands dry for intervals of time, drip rings come in several different forms. For take-apart paddles, the rings simply slide onto the shaft into position about six or so inches (15 cm) from the base of the blade. On a single-piece paddle the drip rings need to be cut, wrapped around the shaft, and spliced in place.

A final paddle add-on to consider is reflective tape. This self-adhesive tape comes in squares that can be cut to shape and put on any smooth surface, including paddles and decks, and even, it is claimed, fabrics such as a PFD. If you occasionally paddle at night, or even have the chance of being out at night, it may be worth considering this safety technique. A flashing pair of paddle blades is often the first sign of a kayaker to be seen by others on the water, and that should be doubly true at night for any vessel using lights.

Spray Skirts

For serious kayaking, the spray skirt or *spray deck* is the most important accessory after the paddle in improving your performance as a paddler. A good quality skirt that fits you and your kayak correctly and remains in place when the water gets rough is indispensable for keeping water out of the cockpit and allowing you to roll and brace with confidence. Like money invested in a good paddle, it pays in the long run to get the best spray skirt you can. Of course, there is no rule you can't have two spray skirts, one for rough conditions and inclement weather and another style for lazy days and protected waters.

Skirt design has improved steadily over the last decade or so. The greatest improvements are how they fit both the kayak and the paddler. Reinforced rubber or Kevlar brands have created bombproof cockpit fits, even on kayaks with large cockpit openings. Neoprene-nylon combination skirts provide a greater range of fit possibilities for the paddler who may be wearing varying layers of protective clothing. Additional features like suspenders or pockets may be advantageous as well in certain applications. For years, I have used a skirt pocket to carry a small emergency kit on trips in remote areas, in the event of being separated from the kayak.

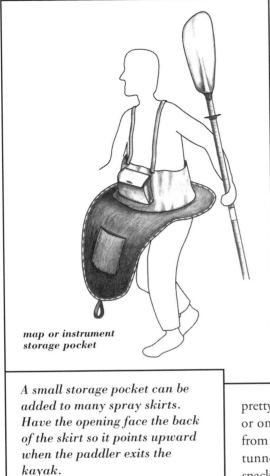

*map or instrument
storage pocket*

*A small storage pocket can be
added to many spray skirts.
Have the opening face the back
of the skirt so it points upward
when the paddler exits the
kayak.*

Finding the right skirt that fits your kayak is the first step. Most kayak manufacturers offer one or several standard spray skirts or spray decks that are designed to fit their models of boats. Also, several specialized makers of skirts, such as Snap Dragon Designs and Palm, build a variety of high-quality styles for most major kayak designs. If you are shopping for a new skirt, be sure to haul your kayak along to assure a good fit.

There is a limit to what you can do to improve an older or very basic skirt that fits poorly or collects water above your lap. For a sagging nylon skirt, it may be possible to add some suspenders to pick up the slack. Using nylon webbing and various plastic buckle components available from outdoor stores, a functional set can be rigged up without doing any sewing. If you are handy with a sewing machine that can handle layers of nylon, a permanent set of suspenders, a better grab loop, or even a pocket could be added.

Adding a pocket to a neoprene skirt is a pretty straightforward project. A simple patch pocket or one with sides for more depth can be fashioned from neoprene material and bonded to the spray skirt tunnel or onto the deck area to hold a radio, GPS, snacks, or some other item you want handy. You may want to face a pocket on the deck area of the skirt with the opening to the back so that it is not upside down when you step out of the kayak and the front of the skirt hangs downward. Use Aquaseal with the Cotol accelerator for bonding purposes.

PFDs

Personal flotation devices for many years were the ugly orange things that you had to have along on outings and maybe even wear sometimes. Like many of the other accessories discussed, PFD design and styling have come a long way in the last few years. The fit of many styles has greatly improved, particularly for wearing over spray skirts, for performance paddling where upper-body flexibility is needed, and for most women. Useful accessories such as mesh pockets, rescue gear attachments, and knife tabs have also helped make PFDs more desirable to wear. Some of these accessories are available as add-ons that may fit on older models of PFDs, so you may be able to customize your old one.

Kayak Flotation

Choosing the best way to outfit your kayak is a matter of balancing weight, cost, and storage needs, but one prime rule should be to fill all unused space with something that floats. A swamped kayak in calm water is a virtually unmanageable hulk, and one in moving water is a deadly missile. Even if you are on a tight budget or are just going for a spin around the local lake, put something that floats in each end of the kayak.

With the multitude of float bags and dry bags available today, organizing a flotation system for any kayak should be easy. These bags come in a range from inexpensive, but heavier, vinyl material to PVC-coated fabrics, to urethane-coated nylon bags that are lighter, more abrasion-resistant, and more expensive. Most kayak manufacturers will distribute flotation sets specifically designed for a given kayak model. You can obtain a wider selection from the actual flotation manufacturers, such as industry leader Voyageur, for fine-tuning your needs.

Outfitting a whitewater kayak with flotation devices is pretty straightforward. Kayaks with support pillars will need split bow and stern sets of a specific length, and some of the latest ultra-short play boats may only have room in the tiny space in front of the foot pegs in the bow for a *rodeo* float bag. The float bags should fill as much of the compartment as possible and fit snugly in place when inflated. When topping off the float bags with air on a cool morning, leave a bit of expansion room inside for a warm sunny day; conversely, make sure the bags will stay snug if the water temperature is a lot colder.

Larger river touring and recreational kayaks usually don't have the pillars and will then need larger, single air bags in the bow and stern. When you get into longer day tours and overnight camping trips, then it is time to add combination storage-flotation bags and other dry bags to the mix, with the goal of filling up all the available space. Storage-flotation bags can be used full or partially empty and will usually come with long air hoses to make filling with air far easier. Dry bags come in many different sizes to match your equipment needs and can be nestled into many different

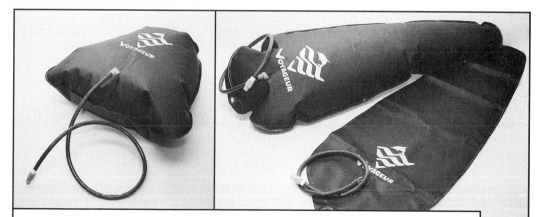

Left: *A rodeo-style kayak bow flotation bag from Voyageur.* Right: *A split stern flotation set from Voyageur. Split sets are necessary on kayaks with installed support pillars.*

Many larger single and tandem kayaks have a lot of extra space that can be filled with flotation for safety in open-water conditions. The area forward of the foot braces and along the sides of the seat are additional spaces to check.

corners. Keep in mind that even a dry bag packed tightly with gear still acts as flotation by displacing water.

Sea kayaks with bulkheaded compartments will have buoyancy as long as the hatches are watertight. In many cases, it is a good contingency plan to keep a dry bag or air bag in these compartments when empty. Hatch covers can be lost, and damage can result in leaks.

For kayaks with large volume cockpits or for kayaks with no bulkheads, an alternative piece of gear, a *sea sock*, can create extra flotation when needed. A sea sock is basically a large sock-like bag of nylon that attaches to the cockpit coaming and lines the inside of the cockpit. The spray skirt fits over the coaming and the sock, and the paddler sits in the bag and braces off the inside contact points as always. The sea sock is held in place by air pressure, and prevents water from filling the farther recesses of the kayak, thereby adding buoyancy. These work especially well in wood-frame kayaks and other kayaks that may be difficult to fill with inflatable bags.

When paddling a large-capacity kayak mostly empty, you may want to carry some extra weight to improve stability and handling in windy conditions. This ballast, whether it be water containers, rocks, or gear, lowers your center of gravity and aids in tracking as well. Keep this weight low and as close to the center of the kayak as possible, with a proportion of the weight somewhere to the front, so as not to affect the bow-to-stern trim. Use your empty float bags or dry bags to wedge the weight firmly in place or come up with a tie-down system so a shifting load doesn't put you in an impossible situation.

Another flotation idea that comes up occasionally is the use of *expanding polyurethane foams* that come in pressurized cans for household use. Unless you know exactly what you are doing, expanding foam is hard to control, can be quite messy, and can generate a lot of pressure that could damage the hull of some boats. I would be very cautious about proceeding with this idea and suspect that a significant amount of the foam would be heavier than a set of float bags. It would be safer to fill the odd spaces here and there with shapes of minicell foam, if you want to be meticulous about maximizing flotation.

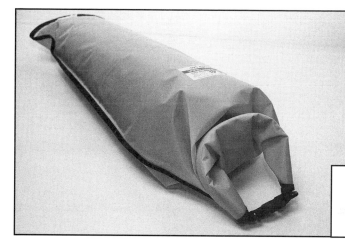

A tapered storage bag with roll-top closure from Cascade Designs.

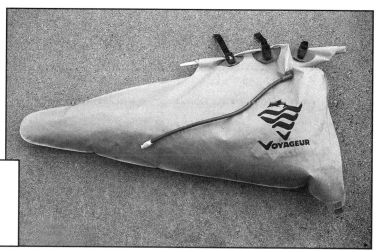

A storage-flotation bag with a hatch-accessible closure from Voyageur.

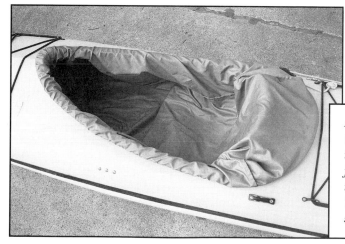

A sea sock is a liner bag that attaches to the coaming and prevents water from getting into the farther recesses of the cockpit. The paddler sits inside the sock and paddles as usual.

Cockpit Covers

Another useful accessory for most kinds of kayaks is the cockpit cover. They keep not only the rain but also small critters out when your kayak is outside. They also make your boat more aerodynamic when transported on the roof of a vehicle. If you transport your kayak right side up as most sea kayaks are, a cover can keep out substantial amounts of rain as well. For serious distance travel, neoprene covers stay on the cockpit better and withstand better the rapid flexing in the wind. On a kayak camping trip, the cover will save on wear and tear to the deck—and a deck compass—by eliminating the temptation to turn the boat upside down at night.

Additional Touring Accessories

Kayak touring and sea kayaking can be a very gadget-intensive sport as innovative paddlers with an inventive streak come up with new and easier ways to do this and that. To keep abreast of the newest innovations, it pays to search the paddling magazines and other sources listed in chapter 8. Keep in mind that even with all these convenient accessories that are sometimes so much fun, the fundamental basis of kayaking remains the kayak, the paddle, the water, and you—and your sound judgment.

MAP AND CHART CASES

A number of good waterproof map cases, small and large, are available to make navigation an easier task. They will last longer if you keep them dried out and use a UV inhibitor on the vinyl surfaces. The inks on some printed materials or photocopies of maps may occasionally stain the inside vinyl surfaces of map cases. To avoid this and to extend the life of the maps and charts, treat maps with a waterproofing designed for maps or with an artist's lacquer spray.

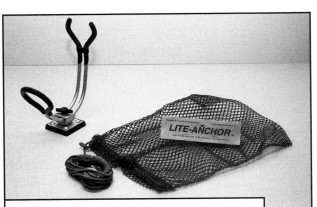

Fishing accessories: A deck-mounted rod holder and a mesh anchor bag that holds rocks are among the many accessories that you can use to adapt kayak touring to your particular needs.

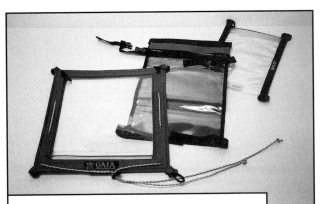

Waterproof map cases from Gaia, Seattle Sports, and Cascade Designs. Treating maps with a liquid waterproofing treatment is still a good idea to prevent damage from condensation and accidental leaks.

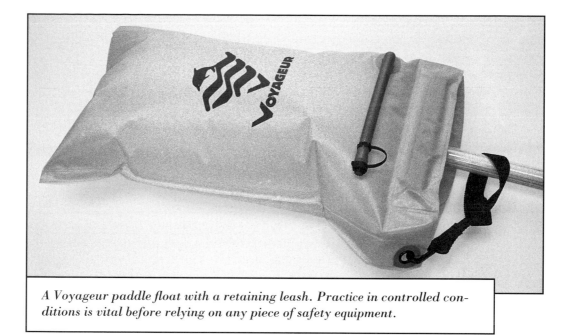

A Voyageur paddle float with a retaining leash. Practice in controlled conditions is vital before relying on any piece of safety equipment.

SELF-RESCUE EQUIPMENT

The foundation for safe paddling is built on strong paddling and boat handling skills and the judgment skills to stay out of trouble in the first place. As a backup, a number of commonly used self-rescue accessories have become standard equipment. Handheld bilge pumps are by far the most popular. They can be used solo or to assist another paddler. Their drawbacks include the possibility of easily losing one and the difficulty of operating such a pump in the types of conditions that may cause a capsize in the first place.

To reenter a kayak after a capsize, the *paddle float* is the commonly carried piece of equipment for self-rescue. These floats utilize a paddle to create an outrigger for stabilizing the

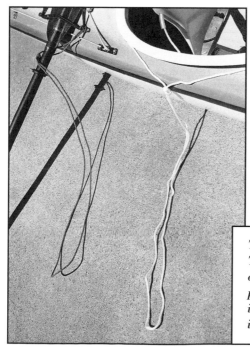

Two methods of rigging a rescue stirrup. The lower one is looped around the cockpit coaming, and the upper one is stabilized by a paddle float setup. The sling hangs down into the water, and you use it to step back into the kayak.

kayak while climbing back in. Most commercially available paddle floats are the inflatable variety because they fold up out of the way easily, but rigid foam floats are gaining in popularity since they don't need to be inflated and will not leak. Designs of both of these types have been improving so that they stay fastened better to the paddle blade and they accommodate more paddle blade shapes. Seats and backrests are available that double as emergency paddle floats.

Another, less commonly used piece of gear that I see as valuable is a *sling* or *stirrup* that can be used in conjunction with a paddle float rescue or with various group rescues. This short 5- or 10-foot (1.5 to 3 m) loop of nylon is easy to rig up in various ways and is set up as a foot step to help a cold or tired paddler climb back into the kayak.

TOWING SYSTEMS

Towing systems are a fundamental piece of rescue gear for guided and organized group paddle tours. There are a number of good towing setups on the market at a variety of prices, with models available for both whitewater paddling and sea kayaking. The best way to learn and evaluate them is through an instructional program or a comparative demonstration at an on-water event. An instructor or trip leader will probably want a deck-mounted system for

maximum towing versatility and comfort on a long haul. For occasional use, the *waist-belt systems* are generally adequate and probably necessary for paddlers in kayaks with rudders to keep the towline from getting caught. The length of line needed varies with the type of wave conditions likely to be encountered. Components should be rugged, with stainless-steel carabiners and other hardware to reduce corrosion.

A kayak tow line that attaches to the cockpit coaming from Mark Pack Works. There are a wide variety of deck-mounted and paddler-worn tow systems; to get your system or systems to work well, seek experienced advice and practice by towing others.

SPECIALIZED SAFETY EQUIPMENT

A number of specialized accessories may be useful in certain applications. Most of these fall in the realm of committed open-water paddling, in which access to the shore may not be possible and immediate help from other members of a group or from a third party may not be likely. Reliance on these pieces of equipment must be looked at as being a bit of a gamble. In other words, have a solid background of experience before experimenting and relying on some of these more esoteric items.

The first category of items is the collection of things used for signaling purposes. Some of these are standard emergency kit accessories such as a whistle or signal mirrors. A whistle can easily be attached to a PFD or paddle jacket with a *lanyard* and may be of use if it isn't too windy and your group understands a few prearranged signals. Signal mirrors require practice and a sunny or hazy day to be effective.

Several types of signaling devices may be required on waters regulated by the coast guards of either the United States or Canada. For night paddling, a bright white light, but not a strobe, must be available for use if other craft are approaching. A good quality waterproof flashlight or headlamp with a halogen or equivalent beam will satisfy this requirement. A Coast Guard–approved, handheld or hand-launched flare set may also be required. These serious pyrotechnics must only be used as directed, or they can cause injury. Also check their expiration dates periodically. Other open-water signaling devices include smoke bombs, water dye markers, and trailing ribbons. The time of day or night, haze, wind, and waves will determine how effective any of these devices will be.

The use of any signaling device assumes that someone is going to see or hear them. If you are in trouble, continue to take active steps to solve your predicament, since your signaling attempts are not guaranteed to work, especially in remote areas. If you are attempting to warn another craft of your position, it is not wise to assume that the other vessel has seen you. You may have a feeling of being very visible out in the open, but in reality a kayak is a very hard thing to spot. The idea that a larger boat or ship has a captain standing on the bridge intently peering out over the endless waves is a myth from a bygone era.

Over the years, a number of inflatable rolling or self-reentry aids have come on the market. Some of these are essentially small rafts or floating seats that inflate with the use of CO_2 cartridges, and these may be useful for emergency reentry tools in rough conditions or as an aid for a group member who has become sick or incapacitated. The key to whether any of these devices is of use to your paddling situation is to practice with the item thoroughly in anticipated conditions before trusting its ability to work for you.

Another specialized open-water tool that has a number of uses is a *sea anchor*, which acts like an underwater parachute when deployed and holds the kayak steady in a fixed position against a strong wind. The Driftstopper, a popular model by Boulter of Earth, can be launched and recovered from the bow of the kayak with a line running from the cockpit position, eliminating a destabilizing retrieval from the side. Other styles of sea anchors may be obtained from marine dealers or fishing supply stores.

By greatly slowing down any backward drift in a strong breeze, the sea anchor can hold one's position for a break or for photography or fishing, or during a squall it can hold the bow into the wind for stability. Sea anchors are useful for holding a kayak well away from the surf zone, shoals,

A Driftstopper sea anchor by Boulter of Earth. The anchor is deployed off the bow by a line from the cockpit, where it sits just below the surface, preventing backward drifting in a steady wind.

Kayak sponsons are flotation bags that add width and stability to the hull in certain conditions. They may be useful for self-rescue, assisting an incapacitated paddler, or for specialized purposes such as fishing, but they require practice and special hardware.

or a dangerous shoreline during a rescue. I have heard of their use as a way to maintain stability in the surf, but I would consider that to be an emergency approach. Too many things can go wrong while paddling in the surf without adding another complex variable. A sea anchor needs a certain amount of depth to function effectively, so it is best to avoid areas where it is shallow enough for the anchor to get hung up on submerged objects.

Kayak *sponsons* are another inflatable rescue and stabilizing accessory that have generated a certain amount of debate. Sponson floats come in a set of two that attach to either side of the cockpit, adding considerable width and stability, so much so that it is even possible to stand up in the kayak. The variety distributed by Voyageur can be rigged into position quickly enough, with a little practice, to be an alternative self-entry method to the standard paddle float procedure. Sponsons also can provide stability for someone in a group who has gotten ill or incapacitated. For quick deployment, however, some deck fittings and buckles need to be installed on the kayak in advance.

In steep or breaking seas, the extra width created by the sponsons may actually be destabilizing if the kayak broaches to the waves. But with the use of a sea anchor to hold the bow into the wind, the sponsons could provide a stable platform that can be used to ride out a storm or to take a needed rest on a long crossing. Several years ago, I practiced with such a setup before a trip with a 45-mile crossing on Lake Superior and strongly recommend that anyone anticipating using a combination of this gear thoroughly practice to get a feel for the limitations of deploying and retrieving the system. Fiddling with lines, buckles, and straps in rough conditions are moments when you cannot be poised to react with the paddle in hand.

The final piece of emergency-related gear that gets mentioned occasionally is the use of something to act as a radar reflector. Round, basketball-sized reflectors are available that are generally used on the masts of sailboats. The consensus on this idea is that any kayak-mounted system is very probably going to be invisible, or very intermittent at best, on any ship's radar.

ELECTRONIC EQUIPMENT AND KAYAKS

Electronic gadgets are increasingly becoming a major part of the equipment repertoire of the serious sea kayaker. Photography has always been a motivating factor in drawing people to the outdoors, and cameras have become more dependent on complex electronics. VHF weather and broadcast radios have become smaller, more affordable, and widespread amongst kayakers. The advent of GPS instruments is revolutionizing the art of navigation. And of course, cellular phones— love 'em or hate 'em—are becoming ubiquitous in the outdoors as well.

As discussed in chapter 4, water, especially salt water, and anything electrical are at best an uneasy mix. How waterproof, submersible, weatherproof, or splash resistant a gadget can be made is an elusive characteristic, and even the best of the best can occasionally fail. Often there is a compromise between the most waterproof construction and the most sophisticated features available, so you may have to prioritize your needs. Other than diving, few other activities require as much waterproofness as sea kayaking.

Cameras are a classic example. You generally will need to give up a number of features, such as interchangeable telephoto lenses, to get a waterproof camera. You can always carry several different cameras; otherwise, it will be necessary to choose between point-and-shoot, here-I-was snapshots, and the once-in-a-lifetime, calendar-quality wildlife photo. The versatility of waterproof and weather-resistant cameras is improving all the time, and the same will eventually be true of digital photography as well.

Technology is racing ahead with GPS features as well, but absolutely reliable waterproof construction is still not quite here. Ease of interaction with map software will be the greatest benefit for kayak navigation, allowing preplanned trip waypoints as well as a post-trip record of the route, and we can only speculate what the future will bring. In the rush to acquire electronic navigational gadgets, don't neglect your classic map and compass skills that remain the foundation of route finding.

VHF frequency handheld marine radios are the preferred means for serious open-water paddlers to monitor weather forecasts, conduct important communications within a group, and contact the outside world in the event of emergencies and overdue returns. These also have varying degrees of waterproofness. The distance a VHF radio can reach is dependent on a line-of-sight connection and on the power output of the unit, so there must be another boater, ship, or land-based station in the vicinity monitoring their radio for a signal to be picked up. Whether you are just looking for an occasional forecast or want to be in constant contact with the rest of the marine world will determine the degree of sophistication you need in a radio system.

The basic three-channel weather radio available from a number of sources provides access to forecasts for a modest price but is not waterproof and does not seem to have the range of the better VHF radio.

Cellular phones are making inroads as an alternative form of emergency communication in the outdoors. Since they are becoming so common for business, personal, and automotive use, it is inevitable that they will show up on kayak tours. Cell phones are great for making quick connections to the outside land-based world, but there are a number of limitations. As of yet, there are no remotely waterproof portable models available that I have heard of, so they need careful protection from the elements. They are also dependent upon being within range of a signal pickup point, although with satellite technology, this will probably change.

As for emergencies, many land-based authorities connected to the 911 system may not be equipped to carry out water-related rescues, although this too will change as links to coast guard and marine rescue facilities are built into the system. A cellular signal does not provide for the ability to locate the position of the caller in the way that a VHF signal can be pinpointed. At this time, a cell phone should be looked on as a supplemental form of communication, mainly good for phoning in changed float plans in relatively populated areas.

With any of this electronic equipment, the degree of waterproofness, or lack thereof, can be made up with the use of watertight storage bags. Some of the radio and GPS distributors may offer such cases with their products. You can get other, and probably better, ones through marine or outdoor sports sources. The degree of versatility and ease of use of your device may be somewhat compromised by the type of protective case needed. This is part of the waterproof issue you will need to weigh when making an investment in a valuable instrument.

6

THE DO-IT-YOURSELF KAYAKER

Over the years, I have known a number of paddlers who seem to spend more time tinkering with their gear, making modifications, and designing new things than actually paddling. These do-it-yourselfers proudly demonstrate what they have done, usually pointing out how little it cost to do their project compared to the commercial alternative. And I think, how many hours did this masterpiece take to complete, and what is one's time worth? Nevertheless, there is great satisfaction in creating something unique in doing the work yourself.

Even though I tend to fall into the let's-just-get-out-there-and-paddle school, I too have had my creative moments of joy from designing and making something that solves a gear problem. For many others with this creative streak, the world of kayaking still offers some unique opportunities for self-expression. This chapter reviews what some of those opportunities are.

Building Your Own Kayak

Judging by the interest that hand-crafted kayaks always generate at paddling events and symposiums, there are a sizable number of kayakers interested in building their own kayaks, or at least who like to dream about it. Wooden-hulled or skin-on-frame kayaks offer a number of advantages, including being relatively light and responsive, and easily customizable and repairable. However, they require more care and maintenance than a kayak made from synthetic materials. And even though on paper the cost of a handmade kayak might appear to be much less than a commercially made one, after factoring in the sweat equity, even at minimum wage levels, the difference may not be all that much.

Nevertheless, the decision to build a boat is ultimately based on pride of workmanship and pride of ownership. If you want a practical handmade craft that meets your paddling needs when you are finished, put the same planning and self-reflection when purchasing a manufactured kayak into choosing the appropriate model to build. Due to the nature of the materials used, most handmade kayaks fall into the recreational touring or sea kayaking end of the kayak spectrum. It will be difficult to modify a design much beyond its intended niche, so shop around for a model that will work for you and your skill level.

Next, assess the creative skills that will be required and be sure you understand the use of all tools and procedures needed to complete the job, or know where to turn for assistance. If uncertain whether or not your abilities are up to the task, consider the option of a kayak-building course or school. If in this latter category, look for a kayak kit with detailed instructions. For more experienced builders, the possibilities are many, with wood-strip kayaks and other more complex techniques being within reach.

Plans, parts, and courses are available for those with an interest in more traditional designs—various skin-on-frame kayaks and *baidarkas* (Inuit-designed kayaks), for example. For information on these different sources, see the resource lists in chapter 8, check the ads and classifieds in the paddlesports magazines, such as *Sea Kayaker*, or do a search of the Internet. Many of the larger canoeing and kayaking clubs have members who are knowledgeable builders.

Whereas much of the focus on building kayaks centers on wood and related materials, low-cost fiberglass kits are available. Also, it is possible to hook up with groups who are still making composite boats (cloth and resin or fiberglass) by hand. This latter group is definitely a small minorit, compared to the pre-polyethylene, garage operations of the 1960s and 1970s. Most composite kayak builders are in pursuit of ultralight slalom and racing designs.

Another option for those who want the aesthetics of hand-crafted kayaks but don't have the time to build one is to consider buying a finished boat or hiring someone to build one. Check local kayak club newsletters, regional kayak fairs or symposiums, or with some of the specialized small boat shops for contacts. Many good builders keep making kayaks for the joy of building and have excellent kayaks for sale or might be willing to make one to your specifications.

One of the advantages of building your own kayak is that you have a certain amount of leeway as to how you outfit the hull and deck. You can decide whether to keep a simple, sleek look on the deck or to add bulkheads and some kind of hatch system. If you want hatches, you can opt for matching wood hatches or a potentially more waterproof commercial setup, such as a *VCP hatch*. You can design a custom-fit seat to maximize your comfort and control over the kayak. If you are going to add a rudder, I recommend using one of the commercially-available kits, although I have seen some fully functional, handmade wooden rudders.

Making a Paddle

Paralleling the interest in traditional and wood kayaks is the growth in popularity of Greenland style paddles. These narrow, *unfeathered paddles* hark back to a number of Inuit designs and require learning a different *paddling cadence* and *method of stroking*. Generally made from one piece of wood, these paddles are very conducive to being handcrafted. Kits and courses are available, and most sea kayak symposiums cover this topic as a regular feature. *Sea Kayaker* magazine has devoted several good articles to this topic, and back issues or reprints are available.

It's possible to make a standard, wide-blade kayak paddle, but such a woodworking project is a bit more complex, requiring laminated pieces and more complex, feathered angles. Check the bibliography (chapter 8) for kayak-building titles that also cover paddle construction.

Building Accessories

In the late 1960s and 1970s, the original boom years of the back-to-nature and outdoor sports movement, good equipment was hard to find, and it seemed that almost everybody tried their hand at making some of their own gear. You could purchase kits for making all sorts of outdoor clothing and sewn goods, and anyone with a sewing machine could save a few dollars and be the envy of the group. Now, the days of being able to duplicate with a home machine the high quality, state-of-the-art commercial gear are mostly gone. Complex, laminated or coated fabrics, heat-taped seams, and combinations of dissimilar materials are beyond the capabilities of the home shop.

Nevertheless, if you are determined to whip up something on your own, you have many options and a plethora of like-minded paddlers. Remember that you don't have to entirely reinvent the wheel—or paddle. Check out the innovations of others by frequenting competitions, rodeos, expos, and symposiums. Here are a few thoughts that might trigger your creative powers.

- **Sewn accessories.** With the right sewing equipment, you can make without too much difficulty spray skirts, cockpit covers, stuff bags, and other nylon items. The trick is to get the patterns exactly right; you want a good fit without a lot of sagging material. In the case of a skirt, there should be enough play in the *tunnel section* to allow for flexibility while *bracing* and *rolling*. Use a good quality, heavy duty, urethane-coated fabric, and then seal the seams thoroughly.

- **Working with neoprene.** Creating accessories such as a spray skirt or cockpit cover from neoprene is tedious but possible. Seams can be glued or stitched and glued in sections. Tolerances on fit will be closer than working with nylon.

- **Deck accessories.** You can handcraft many different deck add-ons, and your imagination is the only limiting factor. *Grab handles* can be fashioned from sections of PVC pipe, *compass mounts* can be molded out of wood, foam, and other materials, and so on. Use only stainless steel or other corrosion-resistant mounting hardware.

You can make a grab handle from a section of PVC piping. Work the knot back into the tube after it's tied.

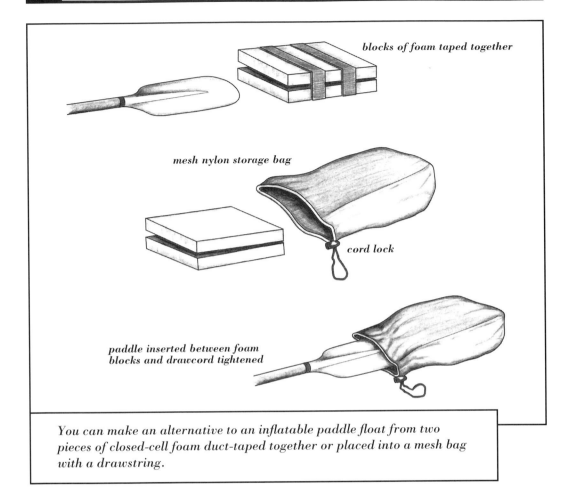

blocks of foam taped together

mesh nylon storage bag

cord lock

paddle inserted between foam blocks and drawcord tightened

You can make an alternative to an inflatable paddle float from two pieces of closed-cell foam duct-taped together or placed into a mesh bag with a drawstring.

- **Safety accessories.** With access to the right components, *throw bags*, *tow ropes*, and other safety gear can be assembled. Obviously, be especially cautious when designing items that will be used in emergency situations and be sure to test them to make sure they will function as intended. Unintentional entanglements can occur when people are under the pressure of an emergency situation and they are using poorly designed equipment. You can devise a foam *paddle float* for kayak reentry using an appropriately sized mesh bag with a drawstring and two pieces of minicell foam cut to fit. Although bulkier than an *inflatable float*, this alternative saves time needed to fill an inflatable with air.

- **Sails and kites.** People have been fascinated for some time with the idea of combining wind power with kayaking. All the different systems for doing this, however, will require modifications to your kayak, and some of these will be major. Masted sails must have a structural support through the deck that is mounted to the hull. Also in order to sail in any direction other than downwind, you will need to install a leeboard system or at least a rudder. Kites can be used for downwind assistance, but plenty of time and space must be allowed for retrieval. You can be pulled hundreds of yards in the time it takes to reel in a kite—enough time to be pulled into the path of a ship or into a dangerous reef.

- **Portaging devices.** If you like tinkering with various materials, you can construct many of the kayak transporting devices discussed in chapter 7 with a little bit of ingenuity and a set of utility wheels. If you are bound for interior wilderness waterways, the portage yoke system described in that chapter is worth serious consideration.

- **Kayak workstand.** The do-it-yourself paddler can choose from a variety of supports for holding kayaks at a working level. Sling arrangements can be hung from a garage or basement rafter, perhaps with a pulley system. Sawhorse kits, available from home improvement stores, can be modified with contoured foam or your car-rack saddle mounts in the off-season to provide a rigid workstation. As illustrated, you can also improvise with carpet and scrap plywood or lumber to make two-piece, take-apart workstands. This latter workstand is especially recommended if work space is limited and seasonal.

One of several easy ways to make a storage or workstand. Padding the edges with carpet scraps or stiff foam will cushion the hull.

7

Cartopping and Transporting Your Kayak

Your kayak is a craft of grace and beauty as you guide it across the water, but once on land, it's a different story. The hardest work of a kayak tour is often at the beginning and end when you must jockey the awkward shape in and out of a garage, on and off a vehicle, and to and from the water's edge. Whatever you can do to reduce the annoyance of hauling will make your paddling experiences more enjoyable and enable you to get onto the water more frequently. This chapter looks at these on-land issues involving hauling to and from the water, portaging, and safely *cartopping* and traveling with your kayak. We also look at security issues—protecting your kayak from theft.

To and From the Water's Edge

There's no getting around the fact that kayaks are awkward and relatively heavy to carry. As discussed, lightweight alternatives are available, but they may not be affordable or practical, so in most cases you will be faced with moving a 40- to 65-pound (18 to 29.25 kg) boat around. First and foremost, be aware of and protect your back while lifting and carrying. Wear and tear on the kayak is cheaper to deal with than pulled muscles and herniated discs. Be familiar with proper lifting and carrying techniques, and take your time.

Moving a kayak around is easiest as a two-person operation. Most kayaks have grab handles or loops, and with one person on each end, away you go. Space permitting, two kayaks can be carried at one time. In a group-paddling situation then, it is good paddling etiquette to offer to team up and get those kayaks moved. This works most comfortably if you don't have a ton of gear already in the kayak, so plan on doing your final packing as close to the water as feasible. Remember to be aware of shifting tides and other boater's needs for access while loading and unloading. Packed gear in a series of dry bags makes this process quick and efficient. If you are new to this game, practice packing your kayak beforehand.

When handling a kayak by yourself, the job gets more awkward. Whitewater kayaks and smaller *day touring kayaks* can be carried by balancing the cockpit coaming on one shoulder, but smaller paddlers may find this method uncomfortable since most polyethylene kayaks equipped with air bags weigh in at over 40 pounds. Longer, asymmetrical touring and sea kayaks are even heavier, and their balance point may not be located at a usable point on the coaming. The down-and-dirty alternative is to grab one end and drag the kayak where you want it to go. This can be hard on the surface of the hull, although dragging a kayak over grass or sand, which I sometimes do, is obviously not as abrasive as the surface of a parking lot. If you have to drag it, keep the kayak flat and low to spread out the wear over a larger surface, rather than dragging it along one of the stems.

Carrying Devices

Several pieces of equipment can enhance the carrying process. I have seen a couple of webbing sling arrangements that in effect provide a large shoulder strap for lifting. Originally designed for surfboards, this sling works for small kayaks as well. It wouldn't be too hard to rig such an arrangement up out of the webbing, buckles, and shoulder pads available at many outdoor stores.

One of the oldest technological innovations—the wheel—has been applied to kayaks as well. There is a small booming market for portaging wheels and carts. I am aware of at least a dozen different styles, and although designed with canoes and larger sea kayaks in mind, there is no reason they can't be applied to smaller kayaks if someone wants the assistance.

Usually developed by entrepreneurial paddlers/inventors who have tried to build a better mousetrap, you can choose from a myriad of styles of portage wheel systems. There are two general types. *End wheels* will fit onto or near the end of the boat and allow it to be wheeled when you pick up the other end. This style is usually small enough to fit in the kayak, but when moving the kayak, you still have to lift one end. *Center wheels* are basically a two-wheel cart that cradles the hull at its balance point. The kayak can then be wheeled around without any lifting

One of many types of kayak portage wheel systems.

needed, by holding onto one of the *grab loops*. These carts are usually too large to easily fit into a kayak, although some models fold fairly flat.

The key to the versatility of these devices is the size of the wheels. Smaller plastic wheels, about 8 inches (20.32 cm) in diameter or less—though the cheapest and most compact—will roll along on smooth surfaces, but will quickly bog down in thick grass, sand, and on obstructions such as curbs. Larger wheels will get you over the curbs and through the softer stuff more easily. Extra features like axles with bearings and pneumatic tires will carry more weight and cover longer distances more smoothly.

If you do any amount of traveling and paddling out of different areas, you'll probably find that a portage device is invaluable. Sometimes parking is not available very close to potential put-in points. Also, access to some of the most spectacular paddling areas in various parts of the continent is solely by commercial ferry boat. Wheeling a kayak on board is much easier than trying to carry a loaded one.

Portage Yokes

There are times and places when wheeled portage devices will not work. You may need to carry a kayak along a narrow trail or over a rough surface where wheels won't roll. Someday you may want to plan a paddling trip to a wilderness area where there are trails connecting various bodies of water. The Boundary Waters/Quetico wilderness area of the Minnesota-Ontario border region is the most well known of these places. I have spent several seasons exploring in a small touring kayak this mazelike network of lakes and rivers. After some trial and error, I learned that the easiest way to carry the kayak was to borrow the technique of the portage yoke from the world of canoeing.

Carrying a kayak, even unloaded, more than a hundred yards or so is a pain on the neck, literally, or in the back, or arms, so I cobbled together a kayak *portage yoke* that works similarly to one designed for canoes. The yoke is basically just a brace, usually padded, that carries the weight of the boat on your shoulders. It is positioned at the balance point of the boat, freeing your arms to do minimal work steadying the hull while you walk. The trick with a kayak, as with a solo canoe, is that the balance point is usually near the seat, so the yoke must be easily removable for paddling.

The kayak yoke I concocted has a set of clamps that allow it to be attached to the cockpit coaming at the kayak's balance point. The coaming, however, must be attached to the kayak with a solid, structural bond to be able to take the weight of the kayak while portaging with a yoke. Since the balance point of the kayak can vary slightly depending on the load inside, the clamps in the yoke are fitted into a slot that allows the distance between them to be adjusted to fit at different positions along the coaming.

Once the yoke is attached to the kayak, you can then portage it as you would a canoe. On most longer, asymmetrically designed touring and sea kayaks, I have found it easier to portage the craft stern first. From under the kayak most of the cockpit and the lower aft deck provide better visibility of the trail. This also helps to keep the rudder, if you have one, out of trouble. In most cases, when carrying camping gear, partially unpacking the kayak helps. A portage pack or dry bag with shoulder straps is useful to have for carrying this extra stuff on the portage. I prefer

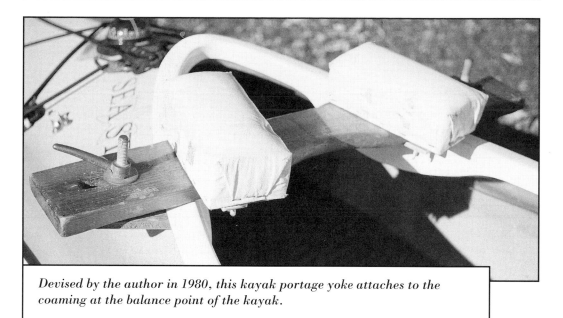

Devised by the author in 1980, this kayak portage yoke attaches to the coaming at the balance point of the kayak.

to carry the pack and the paddle over the portage first, to scout out the route for the kayak carry, but others I know prefer to get the hardest chore—carrying the boat—done first.

Now, the majority of you paddlers are probably thinking that you would have to be crazy to want to carry a kayak around in the woods when it is so much easier to paddle them, and sometimes I have to agree. But for those unforeseen wilderness situations, portaging with a yoke enables access to otherwise inaccessible places.

Cartopping

There are two parts to this discussion. First, we will look at the various systems that can be used to hold and transport one or more kayaks on your vehicle. Then we will discuss the problems of getting kayaks up onto these racks without breaking your back. Setting up a workable, secure rack system and developing some easy techniques for lifting the kayak will make the sport more enjoyable and worth doing more often.

Car Rack Systems

Unless you are one of the rare paddlers who lives on the body of water where you always paddle, you are going to have to transport your kayak at some point via motor vehicle. (Yes, bicycle-pulled trailers for paddlecraft are available, and yes, folding kayaks are an alternative.) This is a piece of paddling equipment in which it pays to invest some time and money into a solid, trouble-free system. Few things can be more disconcerting than to see in the rear-view mirror your new $1,000 kayak go cartwheeling off, loosely connected to a set of $10 closed-cell foam blocks, into the highway median. Worse is to watch it go cartwheeling off into the windshield of a van full of lawyers.

In fact, it pays to have a workable plan in place, preferably attached securely to vehicle roof, before you head off to buy a kayak, so that you can get the boat safely home.

Commercially available rack systems run the spectrum from simple sets of foam blocks and tie-down straps costing $10 to $20 all the way to sophisticated multisport hauling systems that can cost hundreds of dollars. No one system is perfect: each has its advantages and disadvantages. To an extent, it is possible to mix and match to get the setup that will work for you. Also, with some tools and a little ingenuity, you can create your own components and save some money.

Before deciding which rack system you want, consider some of the forces that will be put on the system in a variety of conceivable driving situations. While zooming down the highway with no headwind or crosswinds, as a cartop ornament, a kayak is a very aerodynamic shape. Interestingly, I have found a kayak to be much more efficient in terms of its effect on gas mileage than a canoe or a roof-mounted bicycle. But when you add the effects of surface winds and the turbulence created by other vehicles, especially large trucks, hundreds of pounds of force can be exerted on boat and roof-mount system from a number of different directions.

Sideways torquing by crosswinds or truck turbulence can cause a kayak hull to do the rumba, slipping and sliding back and forth on a roof or crossbar, loosening even the best of tie jobs. For this reason, some sort of lateral support such as a cradle or saddle or vertical post is strongly recommended. Good lateral support should transfer these forces directly to the roof mounts, which in turn must be able to withstand the sideways torque of outside forces.

Vertical wind can create lift and bucking motions, loosening tie-down ropes and possibly damaging a lightweight composite or wood frame hull. These forces can be controlled by placing the supporting crossbars and/or cradle mounts as far apart, toward the ends of the kayak, as possible. In most cases, the use of bow and stern tie-down lines is also necessary to control vertical force. Tied directly to the front and rear bumpers, these lines provide further backup security independent of the roof racks.

Also, a roof-mount system needs to withstand the forward force of sudden deceleration, as in an emergency stop. You do not want your kayak to sail ahead into the rear window of that van of lawyers, now in front of you.

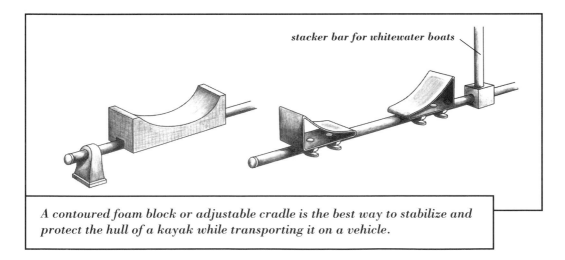

stacker bar for whitewater boats

A contoured foam block or adjustable cradle is the best way to stabilize and protect the hull of a kayak while transporting it on a vehicle.

Clearly, you need to do more than just put the boat onto an old blanket on the roof of the car and tie it down with a piece of clothesline. The various alternatives, listed roughly by cost, include foam block tie-down kits, modifications to existing vehicle luggage racks, commercial sport-rack crossbars with do-it-yourself cradles, and the complete sport rack with manufactured accessories.

Consider cheap foam-block kits only as an emergency or short-distance alternative to a serious roof-mount system. Smaller size foam blocks designed to fit onto a *gunwale* or coaming can pop or roll out of their intended position and quickly blow away. Longer saddle-shaped blocks that tie down are better, and those with a no-skid surface on the bottom provide even more security. Cheap braided polypropylene rope is difficult to tie and keep tight; use a good quality line with a softer hand, and learn the *trucker's hitch* to produce a secure bow and stern line. The weak point of such basic setups is the prevention of lateral slipping. When employing a foam block set-up, avoid fast turns or freeway speeds on windy days.

Stock vehicle luggage racks potentially can provide a better load-carrying arrangement. Keep in mind that many of these racks are not much more than ornamental fixtures and may not tolerate a lot of weight-twisting motion at high speeds. Check the vehicle manufacturer's specifications if possible before relying on the strength of luggage racks. Several distributors of foam-block mounts have models that snap onto standard racks. Make sure they fasten snugly in place, or rig up a backup tie-down. Multisport rack manufacturers offer accessory clips in order to adapt their saddles and other add-ons to luggage racks.

For most cars, vans, and sport utilities, the most secure method of roof mounting a boat will be with one of the commercially available sport rack systems. For years Yakima, of California, and Thule, a Swedish company, have dominated this market. However, there are alternatives, even several pickup truck mounted systems. Because modern streamlined vehicles have few places to solidly mount anything onto, rack manufacturers have risen to the engineering challenge of designing an upright support that firmly attaches to a door frame or other edge without marring the finish.

When properly adjusted, these uprights and crossbars can deal with all the stresses and problems of headwinds, crosswinds, and sudden stops. There are some exceptions; however, these upright systems may not properly fit small two-door cars and convertibles. Older vehicles with traditional rain gutters tend to work well with these systems as well as with the tried-and-true Quik-N-Easy mounts. This additional alternative can be adapted to many uses.

Once upright mounts and the crossbars are securely in place, you can accessorize with the type of kayak holder you want. Whitewater kayaks are often loaded

A Yakima roof rack and saddle-style kayak carrier that has withstood 170,000 miles and six Minnesota winters.

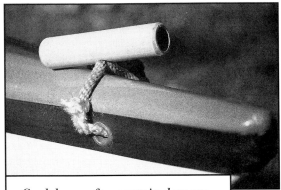

Grab loops often sustain damage from lines used for cartopping.

on their sides, which provides a more rigid shape against the crossbars when tied down. This arrangement also allows for sideways stacking, allowing more boats to fit on one rack, and helps with shuttling back and forth along the river. A set of vertical posts is mounted to rack crossbars against which to tie kayaks.

Polyethylene-hull kayaks, either whitewater or touring, with relatively flat decks can be carried upside down on the crossbars, preferably padded to reduce distorting the decks. Too much tie-down force and the heat from the sun can also deform the shape of the polyethylene. A set of shaped cradles or saddles to hold the boat snugly and spread the load from the tie-down straps provides a kinder and gentler ride for any kayak. Sea kayaks and other more fragile kayaks ride best in their upright positions so that the thicker, more rigid hull takes most of the stress. Use a cockpit cover to avoid taking on a significant load of rainwater during a rainy drive.

Tie the kayak into position with a good-quality *polypropylene rope*, which will stretch much less than nylon when wet and reduce the need for adjustments. Better yet are straps with corrosion-resistant *camming buckles*. These are easier and faster to use and provide a snugger load. When driving any distance, make sure that any loose items in the cockpit and loose parts such as rudder blades are secured to prevent loss or damage from high-speed winds. Schedule periodic stops to double-check the load and help to prevent any unpleasant surprises.

Bow and stern lines are almost always advisable to provide additional load security, but watch for wear and tear on the grab handle loops, which may be taking a lot of force and rope friction. Also, don't let your exuberance with the mechanical force of a trucker's hitch knot deform the hull of your polyethylene kayak or cause stress fractures of your composite boat's gelcoat.

Loading and Unloading

The chore of getting the kayak onto and off the roof of your vehicle is awkward at best and may be fairly impossible for some smaller paddlers. When you don't have extra help available, you can make the chore easier by utilizing various techniques and gimmicks. First, sometimes smaller and simpler is better. As discussed earlier, the efficiency of lightweight kayaks is most noticeable when you are lifting and carrying them around. Shorter, simpler, and lighter kayaks will satisfy most paddler's needs on relatively short day trips and afternoon jaunts. Also, smaller cars are easier to reach the top of and are perfectly capable of hauling most kayaks around. The money saved by opting for an economical vehicle can more than pay for an ultralight composite or wood frame boat.

Two other alternatives to lifting are worth considering. On occasion I have seen small boat trailers rigged up and being used to carry one or two canoes or kayaks. If you don't mind maneuvering a trailer around, the lifting would be minimal. Single boat trailers designed to be pulled behind a bicycle are available. Don't overlook the potential alternative of owning a folding kayak. Being condensed into a more manageable pack, these kayaks solve the issue not only of lifting but also of travel. You can eliminate the need for using a motor vehicle entirely by using public transportation to reach many different paddling destinations, local and far away.

With that said, there are still other ways to get boats up onto roof racks. One option is to carry a sturdy step stool that gives the necessary height to lift, reach, and tie down. Further, lifting one end of the kayak onto the vehicle, and then sliding or hoisting the other end up so that you are never lifting all the weight of the boat at once is a useful technique. Yakima makes a rack accessory mount with built-in rollers, enabling you to glide the kayak into position from the front or back of the vehicle. Then the rollers are latched into place to prevent further movement.

For years, I have used a similar over-the-end sliding method of getting the kayak into place on the roof rack. Since commercially made kayak saddles and foam cradles usually come with grippy rubber surfaces to prevent sliding. I wrap the saddle surface with a set of slippery, nylon-covered pads, which are secured with Velcro. Then the kayak slides into place easily, and once strapped down, remains securely in the saddle, making removal of the nylon slip pads unnecessary. If you are concerned about the kayak hull touching or scratching the back of the roof or hood during this process, a small square of old carpet with rubber backing can be set over that spot while loading.

Another device I have seen but not tested is an extender bar that is positioned to stick out beyond the side of the vehicle from one of the roof-rack crossbars. After placing the kayak parallel to the vehicle, one end of the kayak is lifted onto one of the extender bars. Then the other end is pivoted up onto the second crossbar or saddle. The first end of the boat is then swung from the extender bar onto the first crossbar, and the extender bar is then removed. Seems logical enough, and most importantly, it avoids having to lift the entire kayak at once.

Of course, you can always go paddling with a friend who will share or do the heavy lifting. Maybe some day someone will invent a hydraulic device that will scoop up a kayak and place it on the roof rack. The important thing is to find a method that works for you, protects your back, and allows paddling to be accessible and fun.

Security Issues

Theft of property is an unfortunate aspect of our society, and kayaks are not immune. A kayak conspicuously mounted on the top of a vehicle is pretty much a sitting duck. Also, potential theft is not necessarily an issue relating to big cities or high crime areas. I have heard of more paddlecraft thefts in places adjacent to popular paddling areas where thieves know the value of a kayak. There are no foolproof solutions, and any security measures you take will discourage the casual thief and hopefully slow down and draw attention to the really determined one.

Two problems quickly arise when trying to lock up a big object like a kayak. The first is to figure out what you can attach a cable lock or chain to on a smooth shape like a kayak, and then the second is to find something on your vehicle can you lock it to. In most cases, a cable or chain needs to run through something to be effective. Grab loops or handles, unless made of steel cable, can be cut too easily. In recent years, some kayaks come with a security loop built

The loose end of the Sherlock kayak cable is shut into one of the vehicle doors to provide some security. Don't forget to lock the doors . . .

A kayak security cable from Boulter of Earth that attaches with loops to the bow and stern.

An automobile steering-wheel lock provides a locking point and theft deterrent for your kayak.

somewhere into the deck, allowing a cable to be passed through. Many commercially installed, molded plastic or fiberglass seats have a space on the side where a cable can slide through. Some of these seats can be readily disassembled, however. Also, using the seat as your lock point will interfere with the use of a cockpit cover while the kayak is locked up, unless you modify the cover.

Another option is to use an automotive steering-wheel lock, such as the Club, clamped onto the cockpit coaming to form a lockable loop. It would be very difficult to get one of these off without doing considerable damage to the coaming.

An alternative method of locking with a cable or chain that avoids the cockpit area is the use of two fixed-circumference loops that fit around the hull about a third of the way up from the ends of the kayak (roughly where the bulkheads of a sea kayak would be). When locked in place, the kayak, with its widest cross-section between the loops, cannot be removed. Several commercial products use this principle. One of them, the Sherlock, comes in lengths for different size kayaks and has an extension that can be locked into the car door for added security.

The other half of the locking equation is finding something on the vehicle to attach the cable to. Most vehicles are as devoid as kayaks of secure options. Multisport roof rack systems have optional accessory locks that prevent removal of the system from the roof. Use the crossbars of this system to lock the kayak. A determined thief might get around this security measure with a crowbar; but if that well equipped, such a thief may also have a cable cutter anyway. With a long enough cable, you can run one end inside the vehicle, lock it to a seat belt post or other solid item, and shut the door. This method, however, aside from being a minor nuisance, may become a drip point for water while driving in the rain. Another outside option is to run the cable to the bumper or one of the hook-down points on the frame underneath.

Boat Insurance

You can back up your own kayak security measures and protect your investment by insuring your gear. If you have renter's or homeowner's insurance, "reasonable" amounts of your paddling and other outdoor gear should already be included, but there probably will be a limit on the coverage of watercraft. Contact your agent to find out what this limit is and also find out how much coverage your policy provides while you are traveling with kayak on top of your vehicle. Additional coverage for your kayak or kayaks can usually be purchased at a reasonable premium of $20 to $50 a year.

You also may want to consider the small, additional premium for replacement insurance, so you don't have to deal with depreciated settlements in the event of a loss. Because insurance agents and claim adjusters often have little idea how expensive paddlesports gear can be, save receipts and other documentation of the value of these possessions to make claim processing easier.

8 RESOURCES

Manufacturers

Here's a limited list of manufacturers from or active in the North American market. My apologies to those I've missed. A search of the magazines and trade groups listed below will turn up more, and of course the World Wide Web offers more search possibilities.

AIRE
P.O. Box 3412
Boise ID 83703
800-247-3432
Fax 1-800-701-AIRE
http://www.aire.com

Betsie Bay Kayak
P.O. Box 1706
Frankfort MI 49635
616-352-7774

Chesapeake Light Craft
1805 George Ave.
Annapolis MD 21401
410-267-0137
Fax 301-858-6335
http://www.clcboats.com

Current Designs
10124 McDonald Park Rd.
Sidney BC

CANADA V8L 5X8
250-655-1822
Fax 250-655-1596
http://www.cdkayak.com

Dagger
P.O. Box 1500
Harriman TN 37748
423-882-0404
Fax 423-882-8153
http://www.dagger.com

Eddyline Kayaks
15466 Ashten Rd.
Burlington WA 98233
360-757-2300
http://eddyline.com

Feathercraft Products
1244 Cartwright St. #4
Vancouver BC
CANADA V6H 3R8

604-681-8437
Fax 604-681-7282
http://www.feathercraft.com

Folbot
P.O. Box 70877
Charleston SC 29415
843-744-3483
Fax 843-744-7783
http://www.folbot.com

Great River Outfitters
4180 Elizabeth Lake Rd.
Waterford MI 48328
248-683-4770
Fax 248-644-4960
http://www.erols.com/rapids/
    GRO

Impex
International/P&H/Pyranha
1107 Station Road

Bellport, NY 11713
516-286-1988 (voice and fax)
http://www.impexkayak.com

Klepper Folding Kayaks
4718 1st St. SW
Calgary AB
CANADA T2G 0A2
800-323-3525
Fax 403-287-2122
http://www.klepper.com

Mariner Kayaks
2134 Westlake Ave. N.
Seattle WA 98109
206-284-8404
http://www.marinerkayaks.com

Necky Kayaks
1100 Riverside Rd.
Abbotsford BC
CANADA V2S 7P1
604-850-1206
Fax 604-850-3197

Northwest Kayaks
15145 NE 90th St.
Redmond WA 98052
425-869-1107
Fax 425-869-9014
http://www.nwkayaks.com

Ocean Kayak
P.O. Box 5003
Ferndale WA 98248
800-8-KAYAKS
Fax 360-366-2628
http://www.oceankayak.com

Old Town Canoe Co.
58 Middle St.
Old Town ME 04468
207-827-5513
Fax 207-827-2779
http://www.otcanoe.com

Pacific Water Sports
16055 Pacific Highway
    South
Seattle WA 98188
206-246-9385
Fax 206-439-9040
http://www.pwskayaks.com

Perception, Inc.
111 Kayaker Way
Easley SC 29641
864-859-7518
Fax 864-855-5995
http://www.kayaker.com

Pygmy Boats
P.O. Box 1529
Port Townsend WA 98368
360-385-6143
http://www.pygmyboats.com

Riot Kayak
CP 63
St. Augustin QB
CANADA G3A 1V9
418-667-0915

Seavivor Folding Boats
576 Arlington Ave.
Des Plaines IL 60016
847-297-5953
http://www.seavivor.com

Seaward Kayaks
R.R.#1, Site 16, C-1
12810 S. Lakeshore Dr.
Summerland BC
CANADA V0H 1Z0
250-494-5239
Fax 250-494-5200
http://www.
    seawardkayaks.com

Seda Products/Nautiraid
P.O. Box 997

Chula Vista CA 92012
619-336-2444
Fax 619-336-2405
http://www.sedakayak.com

Sevylor USA
6651 E. 26th St.
Los Angeles CA 90040
323-727-6013
Fax 323-726-0481

Superior Kayaks
P.O. Box 355
Whitelaw WI 54247
920-732-3784

Walden Paddlers
152 Commonwealth Ave.
Concord MA 01742
978-371-3000
Fax 978-371-3012
http://www.members.aol.
    com/waldenpad

Wave Sport
P.O. Box 5207
Steamboat Springs CO 80477
970-736-0080
Fax 970-736-0078
http://www.wavesport.com

Wilderness Systems
P.O. Box 4339
Archdale NC 27263
336-434-7470
Fax 336-434-6912
http://www.wildsys.com

**Wildwasser Sport USA/
    Prijon**
P.O. Box 4617
Boulder CO 80306
303-444-2336
Fax 303-444-2375

Accessories

Space doesn't permit a complete list of the many good manufacturers and distributors of kayaking accessories. For the latest information, browse through the periodicals listed later in this chapter.

AquaBound Technology
19077-95A Ave.
Surrey BC
CANADA V4N 4P3
604-882-2052
Fax 604-882-9988
http://www.aquabound.com
(Whitewater and touring
  paddles)

Boulter of Earth
46 Sussex Road
Washington TWP NJ 07675
201-722-0033
(Driftstopper sea anchors and
  security cables)

**Blue Magic Products, Inc./
  Tectron**
P.O. Box 4175
Stockton CA 95204
800-289-2583
Fax 209-465-5896
(Fabric care products)

Cascade Designs
4000 First Ave. S.
Seattle WA 98134
800-531-9531
Fax 206-505-9525
http://www.cascadedesigns.com
(Dry bags and other kayaking
  and camping accessories)

Deep Sea, Inc.
18935 59th Ave. NE
Arlington WA 98223
360-435-6696
Fax 360-435-4314
(Wetsuits, boots, and gloves)

Doctor D Paddles
80 Second St.
South Portland ME 04106
800-295-0042
Fax 207-741-2477
http://www.maloneofmaine.com
(Wood and synthetic paddles)

Epic Paddles
6657 58th St. NE
Seattle WA 98115
206-523-6306
Fax 206-524-4888
http://www.epicpaddles.com
(Performance kayak paddles)

Grey Owl Paddles
62 Cowansview Rd.
Cambridge ON
CANADA N1R 7N3
519-622-0001
Fax 519-622-0723
(Kayak Paddles)

Kokatat
5350 Ericson Way
Arcata CA 95521
800-225-9749
Fax 707-822-8481
http://www.kokatat.com
(Paddle clothing and dry suits)

Lightning Paddles
22800 S. Unger Rd.
Colton OR 97017
503-824-2938
Fax 503-824-6960
http://www.paddles.com
(Whitewater and touring
  paddles)

Lotus Designs
1060 Old Mars Hill Highway
Weaverville NC 28787
828-689-2470
Fax 828-689-2521
http://www.lotusdesigns.com
(PFDs)

Mark Pack Works
230 Madison St.
Oakland CA 94607
510-452-0243
Fax 510-452-3022
(Sea kayaking accessories)

McNett Outdoor
Box 996
Bellingham WA 98227
360-671-2227
Fax 360-671-4521
(Aquaseal and other repair
  products)

Mitchell Paddles
RR 2, Box 922
Canaan NH 03741
603-523-7004
Fax 603-523-7363
(Whitewater and touring
  paddles)

Mountain Surf
276 Maple St.
Friendsville MD 21531
301-746-5389
Fax 301-746-4089
http://www.mountainsurf.
  com
(Paddling clothing and
  spray skirts)

MTI
P.O. Box 1045
Watertown MA 02272
617-926-0038
Fax 617-926-0325
(PFDs)

Nikwax
P.O. Box 1572
Everett WA 98206
206-303-1410
Fax 206-303-1242
http://www.nikwax-usa.com
(Fabric care products)

North Shore, Inc.
4 Fourth Street
Hood River OR 97031
800-800-7237
Fax 541-386-1982
http://www.nsipadz.com
(Kayak outfitting accessories)

Paddle Boy Designs
1407 Park Ave.
Winona Lake IN 46590
219-268-0081
Fax 219-268-0081
(Kayak portage carts)

Planetary Gear
6350 Gunpark Drive
Boulder CO 80301
303-581-0518
Fax 303-581-9288
(Paddling clothing and outfitting accessories)

Primex of California
P.O. Box 505
Benicia CA 94510
800-422-2482
Fax 707-746-0493
http://www.deluge.com
(Kayak touring accessories)

Rapid Style, Inc.
4300 Howard Ave.

Kensington MD 20895
301-564-0459
Fax 301-564-9268
http://www.erols.com/rapids
(Paddling clothing and spray skirts)

Salamander Paddle Gear
P.O. Box 1363
Bend OR 97709
541-388-1821
Fax 541-388-1831
http://www.
salamanderpaddlegear.com
(Kayak rescue and other accessories)

Sawyer Paddles
299 Rogue River Pkwy.
Talent OR 97540
541-535-3606
Fax 541-535-3621
(Whitewater and touring paddles)

Seattle Sports
1415 NW 52nd St.
Seattle WA 98107
800-632-6163
Fax 206-241-0615
(Dry bags and other boating accessories)

Snap Dragon Design
14320 NE 21st St. #15
Bellevue WA 98007
425-957-3575
Fax 425-957-4547
(Whitewater and touring spray skirts)

Stohlquist Waterware
P.O. Box 3059
Buena Vista CO 81211
800-535-3565
Fax 719-395-2421
http://
stohlquistwaterware.com

(Paddle clothing, PFDs, rescue gear, and spray skirts)

UCO Corp.
9225 151st Ave. NE
Redmond WA 98052
888-297-6062
Fax 425-883-0036
http://www.ucocorp.com
(Kayak parts and camping accessories)

Voyageur/Mad River
P.O. Box 207
Waitsfield VT 05673
802-496-3127
Fax 802-496-6247
http://www.
madrivercanoe.com
(Flotation, dry bags, PFDs, and rescue and outfitting accessories)

Werner Paddles
P.O. Box 1139
Sultan WA 98294
800-275-3311
http://www.
wernerpaddles.com
(Whitewater and touring paddles)

W. L. Gore & Associates, Inc.
P.O. Box 729
Elkton MD 21921
800-431-GORE
Fax 410-392-3849
http://www.gorefabrics.com
(Gore-Tex fabric support and maintenance products)

Yakima Products
1385 8th St.
Arcata CA 95521
888-925-0703
Fax 707-826-8129
http://www.yakima.com
(Car racks and accessories)

Repair Services and Specialized Suppliers

Rainy Pass Repair, Inc.
5307 Roosevelt Way NE
Seattle WA 98105
800-733-4340
Fax 206-523-2864
(Gore-Tex repairs)

Thrifty Outfitters
309 Cedar Ave.
Minneapolis MN 55454

800-866-3162
Fax 612-339-7249
(Gore-Tex repairs)

System Three Resins
P.O. Box 70436
Seattle WA 98107
800-333-5514
http://systemthree.com
(Resins and adhesives)

Gougeon Brothers, Inc.
P.O. Box 908
Bay City MI 48707
517-684-7286
Fax 517-684-1374
http://www.westsystem.com
(West System epoxies)

Paddlesports Associations

These organizations provide valuable and interesting information about the paddlesports scene, including safety and where to find outfitters, retailers, and consumer events.

**American Canoe
    Association**
7432 Alban Station Blvd.,
    Suite B-226
Springfield VA 22150
703-451-0141

American Whitewater
1430 Fenwick Lane
Silver Spring MD 20910

Phone/Fax 301-589-9453
http://www.awa.org

**Professional Paddlesports
    Association**
P.O. Box 248
Butler KY 41006
606-472-2205
Fax 606-472-2030
http://www.propaddle.com

**Trade Association of
    Paddlesports (TAPS)**
12455 No. Wauwatosa Rd.
Mequon WI 53097
414-242-5228
Fax 414-242-4428
http://www.gopaddle.org

Mail-Order Sources

Campmor
P.O. Box 700
Saddle River NJ 07458
800-230-2151
http://www.campmor.com

L.L. Bean
Casco St.
Freeport ME 04033
800-441-5713
http://www.llbean.com

Nantahala Outdoor Center
13077 Hwy. 19 W
Bryson City NC 28713
800-367-3521
Fax 828-488-2498
http://www.nocweb.com

Northwest River Supplies
2009 S. Main St.
Moscow ID 83843
800-635-5202
Fax 208-883-4787
http://www.nrsweb.com

Piragis Northwoods Co.
105 N. Central Ave.
Ely MN 55731
800-223-6565
http://www.piragis.com

Recreational Equipment, Inc.
P.O. Box 2000
Sumner WA 98352
800-426-4840
http://www.rei.com

Internet Mailing Lists and Newsgroups

Don't get enough e-mail? Join a discussion group to keep up on the lively debates in the paddling community.

rec.boats.paddle
A wide-ranging discussion group on paddling topics, heavily used by whitewater enthusiasts.

rec.boats.building
Boatbuilding topics.

PaddleWise Paddling Mailing List
A discussion group covering all aspects of paddling, primarily used by touring and sea kayakers.
Submissions:
paddlewise@lists.intelenet.net

Subscriptions:
paddlewise-request@lists. intelenet.net
http://www.gasp-seakayak.org/ paddlewise/

Magazines

American Whitewater
P.O. Box 636
Margretville NY 12455
914-586-2355

Canoe & Kayak
10526 NE 68th, Suite 3
Kirkland WA 98033
800-692-2663
http://www.canoekayak.com
(Annual buyer's guide issue has comprehensive listing of paddlesports manufacturers)

Ocean Paddler
P.O. Box 314
Bolton D.O. Lancashire
ENGLAND BL5 2FS
Tel./Fax 44 + 01942 842204

Paddler
P.O. Box 775450
Steamboat Springs CO 80477
970-879-1450
Fax 970-870-1404
http://www.
        aca-paddler.org/paddler

River
P.O. Box 1068
Bozeman MT 59771
877-582-5440
Fax 406-582-7667
http://www.rivermag.com

Sea Kayaker
7001 Seaview Ave. NW,
        Suite 135
Seattle WA 96117
206-789-1326
Fax 206-781-1141
http://www.seakayakermag.com

Books and Articles

General Kayaking Information

Diaz, Ralph. *Complete Folding Kayaker*. Camden ME: Ragged Mountain Press, 1994. The most complete work on folding kayaks.

Harrison, Dave. *Sea Kayaking Basics*. New York: Hearst Marine Books, 1993. A general introduction to sea kayaking.

Kellog, Zip, ed. *The Whole Paddler's Catalog*. Camden ME: Ragged Mountain Press, 1997. A source for all kinds of paddling information and trivia.

Kuhne, Cecil. *The Kayaking Sourcebook: A Complete Resource for Great Kayaking on Rivers, Lakes, and the Open Sea*. Old Saybrook CT: Globe Pequot Press, 1998. Lots of leads for further information.

Stuhaug, Dennis. *Kayaking Made Easy: A Manual for Beginners with Tips for the Experienced*. 2nd ed. Old Saybrook CT: Globe Pequot Press, 1998.

Kayak Building

Brinck, Wolfgang. *The Aleutian Kayak: Origins, Construction, and Use of the Traditional Seagoing Baidarka*. Camden ME: Ragged Mountain Press, 1995. Detailed plans for building an Aleutian kayak replica.

Kulczycki, Chris. *The Kayak Shop: Three Elegant Wooden Kayaks Anyone Can Build*. Camden ME: Ragged Mountain Press, 1993. Detailed discussion and plans with lots of photos for three seaworthy touring kayaks.

Putz, George. *Wood and Canvas Kayak Building*. Camden ME: International Marine, 1990. Discussion and plans for making a fabric-covered Greenland kayak.

Rasmussen, Ken. "High Performance Cockpit Layout." *Sea Kayaker* (Feb. 1998). A great description of how to make a well-fitting kayak seat from minicell foam.

Schade, Nick. *The Strip-Built Sea Kayak: Three Rugged, Beautiful Boats You Can Build*. Camden ME: Ragged Mountain Press, 1998. Discussion and plans for building three wood-strip sea kayaks, including one double.

Sea Kayaking Skills

Broze, Matt, and George Gronseth. *Sea Kayaker's Deep Trouble: True Stories and Their Lessons from* Sea Kayaker *Magazine*. Ed. Christopher Cunningham. Camden ME: Ragged Mountain Press, 1997. This is a must-read for a serious and sobering perspective of open-water safety.

Burch, David. *Fundamentals of Kayak Navigation*. 2nd ed. Old Saybrook CT: Globe Pequot Press, 1994. The most complete and definitive discussion of kayak navigation and route planning.

Dowd, John. *Sea Kayaking: A Manual for Long Distance Touring*. Seattle: University of Washington Press, 1988. The classic work on open-ocean paddling.

Foster, Nigel. *Nigel Foster's Sea Kayaking*. 2nd ed. West Sussex, England: Fernhurst Books, 1997. A detailed look at intermediate and advanced sea kayaking technique with many good illustrations and photos.

Hanson, Jonathan. *Complete Sea Kayak Touring*. Camden ME: Ragged Mountain Press, 1998.

Hutchinson, Derek. *The Complete Book of Sea Kayaking*. 4th ed. Old Saybrook CT: Globe Pequot Press, 1995. One of the classics of sea kayaking literature. Packed with information and fun to read.

Johnson, Shelley. *Sea Kayaking: A Woman's Guide*. Camden ME: Ragged Mountain Press, 1998. The perfect resource for beginner kayakers looking for a novel way into the sport.

Seidman, David. *The Essential Sea Kayaker: A Complete Course for the Open Water Paddler*. Camden ME: Ragged Mountain Press, 1992.

Whitewater Topics

Bennett, Jeff. *The Essential Whitewater Kayaker: A Complete Course*. Camden ME: Ragged Mountain Press, 1999.

Lessels, Bruce. *Whitewater Handbook*. 3rd ed. Boston: Appalachian Mountain Club Books, 1994.

Soares, Eric, and Michael Powers. *Extreme Sea Kayaking*. Camden ME: Ragged Mountain Press, 1999. What to read to stretch your kayaking adventures.

Walbridge, Charles, and Wayne Sundmacher Sr. *Whitewater Rescue Manual: New Techniques for Canoeists, Kayakers, and Rafters*. Camden ME: Ragged Mountain Press, 1995. One of the definitive sources for whitewater safety and rescue techniques.

Related Outdoor Topics

Getchell, Annie, and David Getchell Jr. *The Essential Outdoor Gear Manual: Equipment Care, Repair, and Selection*. 2nd ed. Camden ME: Ragged Mountain Press, 2000. An excellent and entertaining source of information about fixing just about any gear.

Seidman, David. *The Essential Wilderness Navigator: How to Find Your Way in the Great Outdoors*. Camden ME: Ragged Mountain Press, 1995.

Index

The Author

ANDY KNAPP is the paddlesports specialist and buyer for Midwest Mountaineering in Minneapolis and a former member of the Board of Directors of the Trade Association of Paddle-Sports (TAPS). The author of numerous articles in *Sea Kayaker*, *Silent Sports*, and other magazines, he is a contributing editor for *Canoe & Kayak* magazine and the editor of the *Upper Midwest Kayak Touring News*. A multisport outdoorsman, he estimates that over the last 35 years he has logged over 123,000 miles biking, kayaking, canoeing, running, snowshoeing, hiking, and skiing.